FRONTPAGE 2002

in easy

MICHAEL PRICE

COMPUTER
STEP

In easy steps is an imprint of Computer Step
Southfield Road . Southam
Warwickshire CV47 0FB . England

http://www.ineasysteps.com

Notice of Liability
Every effort has been made to ensure that this book contains accurate
and current information. However, Computer Step and the author
shall not be liable for any loss or damage suffered by readers as a
result of any information contained herein.

Trademarks
Microsoft® and Windows® are registered trademarks of Microsoft
Corporation. All other trademarks are acknowledged as belonging to
their respective companies.

Printed and bound in the United Kingdom

ISBN 1-84078-144-0

Contents

Enhancing the web 55

4

Finalise the web 71

5

Publishing the web 87

6

Introducing FrontPage 2002

FrontPage 2002 allows you to create and manage websites for personal or business use. This chapter will introduce the use of web space, discuss the features of FrontPage 2002 that help you build and use websites and show you how to install the software.

Covers

Chapter One

The Internet

Send and receive documents, emails, data, device drivers, images or sounds, to a web server or to another user.

You can use the Internet in many different ways. At its simplest, it is a mechanism for exchanging mail with anyone else who has direct or indirect access to the Internet.

A web page is defined using the HTML mark-up language. The page can contain many elements, including text, pictures, sound and video.

To make this easier, the Internet has evolved a format for publishing information, known as the web page. The Internet provides access to millions of web pages, stored on thousands of computers (web servers). The web pages are linked together in groups known as websites. Each website has a unique address (Universal Resource Locator or URL) that allows you to access the primary home or welcome page for the site. Web pages usually refer to other web pages with relevant, related contents.

Use the search engines on the Internet to look for websites and web pages by content, then follow links to other pages and other sites.

1 Search engine

2 UCAS website
With links to:

3 Student Loans
Company site

4 University of Warwick

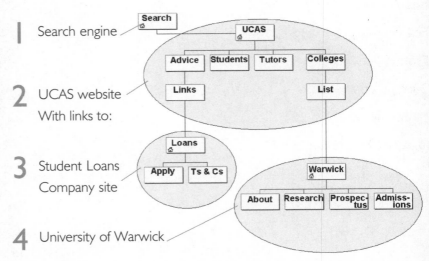

Internet access

You can create a dial-up connection between your PC and the Internet, using a modem and a telephone line. You make the connection when you need to transfer mail or to access information. The connection exists just for the period of the Internet session. The link is made to the web server belonging to your ISP, but once you have dialled in, you can run Internet navigation software, such as Netscape or Internet Explorer, to view documents.

This is the most economical method for less frequent usage, since the set up costs for the modem and the telephone line rental are relatively low, and you pay only for the times when your connection is active. The telephone line is available for other purposes such as fax or voice when you are not using the Internet. You can minimise the time you spend connected, if you increase the capacity of the dial-up connection by choosing a higher speed modem (up to 56 Kbps), or by switching to the digital ISDN type of connection (for 64 Kbps or 128 Kbps).

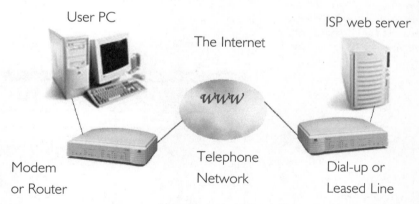

User PC

The Internet

ISP web server

Modem
or Router

Telephone
Network

Dial-up or
Leased Line

For higher rates, or when you want to make your data directly accessible from the Internet, you need a leased line. This provides a dedicated connection that is permanently available. The capacity of the line (the bandwidth) can be chosen, and ranges from 64 Kbps to 2 Mbps or more. The leased line can be rented on a fixed fee, based on the capacity, or charged by usage – the amount of data sent over the line.

ADSL is now becoming available, as a high speed (500 Kbps to 2 Mbps) alternative to ISDN or leased line connections.

Personal home pages

You can create and manage your own website, and be part of the information resource provided on the Internet.

You don't need a website to browse the Internet and search for information, but having your own website does allow you to make your own contribution to the Internet. You may create a personal home page, where you can store links to other websites and web pages that you often want to visit. You can add information to this page or add additional pages, to share with other users on the Internet.

If you have programs, pictures or other data that you would like to share, you can also add these. Soon your home page will develop into a website in its own right, that other users will enjoy visiting.

You can include more features such as a hit counter to record visits and a guest book to record comments. If you are in business of any type, you can use your website to inform others about your goods and services, and give them the opportunity to define their requirements and place their orders.

The personal home page is often used to gain experience with the Internet, and help you plan how to use the Internet to support your business or service.

A typical home page will contain:

Data about the author   Information about the website   Links to bookmarks and other websites

You may also find adverts, banners and pop-up windows – to qualify the site for "free" web resources.

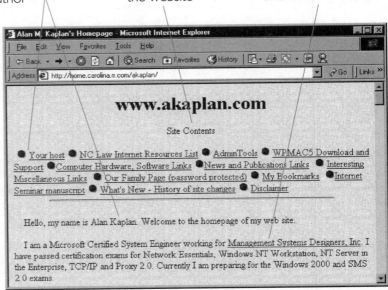

There may be items such as last update or Visits Counter at the bottom.

Web space

You can find extra free web space, but using this means that your website must carry various types of adverts and banners.

The disk storage or web space occupied by the website on the server may be provided by the Internet Service Provider. Most ISPs include 5 MB or 10 MB of web space free, when you subscribe to their Internet connection service. This is sufficient for personal use, but the bigger or more complex your website, the more web space you will require, so you may need to purchase additional capacity.

For individuals and smaller businesses starting out on the Internet, the ISP web servers provide all the necessary functions.

If your ISP does not provide space, or if you have a larger business need, you may choose one of the web hosting services with web space and connection functions. There are also Web Presence Providers (WPPs), who specialise in web hosting. The actual connection is provided by your ISP.

For more advanced corporate websites requiring larger space, dedicated servers may be required. These will be managed at a data centre, with direct highspeed access to the Internet.

Microsoft provides lists of Internet service providers, for personal, small business and corporate users. You can find the latest versions of the lists for the UK at:

http://www.microsoft.com/uk/nextsteps/isp.htm

Your Internet address

Your personal home page will be identified by the server or network domain name, the web space folder name and the web page name. For example, if you use a Dial Pipex ISP account, your web space would have URLs of the form:

http://dialspace.dial.pipex.com/town/plaza/myid/

Server name   Web space folder   User ID

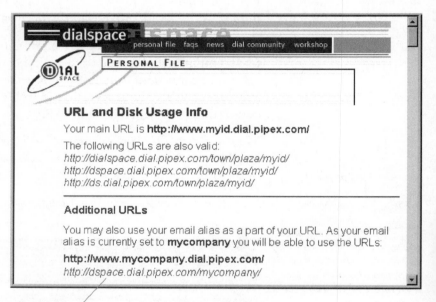

dialspace   personal file   faqs   news   dial community   workshop

PERSONAL FILE

URL and Disk Usage Info

Your main URL is **http://www.myid.dial.pipex.com/**

The following URLs are also valid:
http://dialspace.dial.pipex.com/town/plaza/myid/
http://dspace.dial.pipex.com/town/plaza/myid/
http://ds.dial.pipex.com/town/plaza/myid/

Additional URLs

You may also use your email alias as a part of your URL. As your email alias is currently set to **mycompany** you will be able to use the URLs:

http://www.mycompany.dial.pipex.com/
http://dspace.dial.pipex.com/mycompany/

The email alias for the account is used to construct a short form synonym for the URL that does not rely on knowing the location of the web space.

Some ISPs allow you to choose an account name which becomes part of the server address. The website for an account called Mycompany on the Freeserve ISP would have this URL:

http://www.mycompany.freeserve.co.uk

Finally, for an annual fee of around $35 you can register your own virtual domain name for web space hosted by a WPP. This would give you a URL such as:

http://www.queensmead.com

FrontPage 2002

FrontPage 2002 allows you to design and build home pages and websites that look professional and include all the functions and features you want, without you having to deal with all the intrinsic details of the underlying HTML code. It also provides help in getting the web pages and data files from your system to your web space on the Internet, or onto your network server if you are designing an Intranet site for use on your local area network.

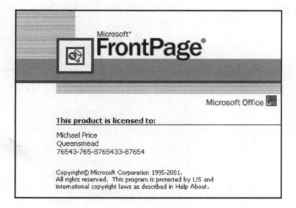

FrontPage 2002 is a tool for both website creation and website management. With it, you can make sure that there is a consistent style and appearance applied to every page. It offers many features, including functions that reside on the server, but you are not restricted to using FrontPage facilities. You can add and change items using native HTML codes and you can incorporate advanced web technologies. It gives you full control over the page, and you can position the items exactly where you want them.

When you have created your website, FrontPage 2002 allows you to set up and maintain it as a unit. You can monitor the status of your site, and apply updates and changes. If you are a member of a workgroup, you can collaborate with other members who are also updating or extending the website.

Because FrontPage 2002 was designed as a part of Office XP, you will find that the processes and procedures are familiar, and you can easily exchange documents and data with the other applications in Office XP.

FrontPage packages

The special edition of Office XP Professional is an upgrade for existing users of Office 2000, and available for a limited period only.

If you already have an existing version of Office, you can obtain FrontPage 2002 as a component of the Office XP Professional Special Edition, which also includes Publisher and the IntelliMouse Explorer optical mouse. FrontPage 2002 is also included in the upgrade edition of Office XP Developer. The other editions of Office XP (Standard and the normal Professional) do not include the FrontPage 2002 application.

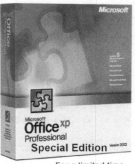

For a limited time

If you do not have a qualifying Office product, you'll need to purchase the full product version of Office XP Developer edition to get a copy of FrontPage included. If you do not need the developer functions, you should install the Office XP Standard or Professional edition, and obtain your copy of FrontPage 2002 as a separate product on its own CD-ROM. As with Office, there will be a full version for new systems, or an upgrade for users of previous versions of FrontPage.

Microsoft offer a free 30-day trial for the Office XP Pro suite. You can also request trials of associated applications, including FrontPage 2002. Details can be found at:

http://www.microsoft.com/ uk/office/eval/

Other Trial Software

You can also order these Office-related products:
 	
• FrontPage 2002
  30-Day Trial CD
  Includes SharePoint
  Team Services

Whether installed stand-alone or part of Office, FrontPage 2002 uses Windows Installer and supports the Microsoft SharePoint Team Services. FrontPage also shares other features introduced in Office XP, e.g. the Task Pane and the multi-item Office Clipboard. It handles automatic web content (headlines, stock ticker and maps) from Microsoft MSN, Expedia and Microsoft bCentral. FrontPage also includes web components such as hit counters, banner ad managers, marquees and hover buttons, and new features such as Photo Gallery, Link Bars and Top 10 Lists.

Requirements

The minimum requirements are not as large, but you'll find webs place high demands on your system, especially if you like lots of animation and video effects.

To use FrontPage 2002, the following components are recommended:

- PC with a Pentium III processor or equivalent.

- Windows 98, Windows Me, Windows 2000 Professional or Windows XP.

- 128 MB memory for Windows 2000 or Windows XP, 64 MB for Windows 98 or Windows Me.

Internet Explorer 5 (or higher) isn't mandatory, but some features won't work without it on your system.

- 165 MB hard disk space, with 115 MB on the hard disk where the operating system is installed (plus additional space for the websites and pages that you will be creating).

- CD-ROM or DVD-ROM drive.

- VGA display adapter (SVGA, 256 colour 800 x 600 or higher recommended).

Have copies of other web browsers, if possible, so you can check out how your site looks from other users' viewpoints.

- Microsoft Mouse, Microsoft IntelliMouse®, or compatible pointing device.

Internet access is needed to use Internet features, so you will need a modem, a cable modem or other mechanism for connecting to the Internet. You'll need a web browser, but it doesn't have to be Internet Explorer, since FrontPage works with any browser.

There will be other components that you need, for Windows or for multimedia applications, including printer, audio adapter, speakers, microphone, scanner or digital camera.

Features of FrontPage

There is an on-going debate between web designers, with the purists preferring HTML, and the pragmatists welcoming tools to relieve the tedium. FrontPage lets you choose the best of both these approaches.

FrontPage 2002 includes many features to make it easier for you to create and manage your website, without having to become involved at a programmer level. It allows you to control the way your pages look, using WYSIWYG (what you see is what you get).

Among the features of FrontPage 2002 are:

Pixel-precise positioning and layering

This allows absolute and relative positioning to place page elements such as graphics and text exactly where needed, using layers to overlap elements.

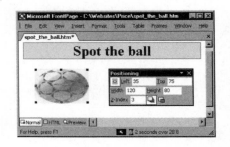

Pre-designed themes

Themes provide ready-made settings for a consistent look across the page and the website. Add your own themes or customize existing themes to suit your preferences (see pages 63–64). Office applications also use FrontPage themes.

You don't need Office XP to use FrontPage 2002, but the two do work hand in hand, since Office applications support HTML as a native file format.

Dynamic HTML

DHTML supports effects such as text and graphics animation and collapsible outlines, which work with Netscape Navigator as well as Internet Explorer.

Cascading Style Sheets

CSS apply consistent formatting, over a related set of pages, or across the whole website.

Office XP integration

FrontPage can integrate data from Office applications. For example, you can incorporate database queries directly into web pages, and even update the database from web pages.

HTML editing

Choose how you want your HTML code stored – what indents, tag colours and capitalization rules to follow – and FrontPage will apply these rules as the code is saved.

If you import web pages, FrontPage 2002 doesn't make changes to existing code except where absolutely necessary.

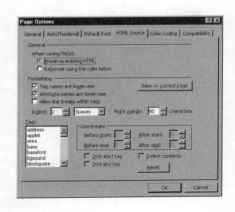

When you edit HTML and scripts from other sources, FrontPage respects the existing structure and layout.

Other coding languages

As well as HTML, you can edit and debug JavaScript and Visual Basic script, and take advantage of pre-built web components and snap-in tools and utilities.

Extend the features of FrontPage to support special applications such as online shopping and e-commerce.

Workgroup support

FrontPage 2002 is not just for individuals. You can work as a group to set up and maintain a shared website. As well as providing the various views, FrontPage eases the task of publishing by letting you flag pages or by sending changed pages only. Tasks such as document updates and hyperlink adjustments are automatically carried out.

Compatibility

You can pre-select which type and version of browser and which type of web server your website will display with. You can also enable or disallow the FrontPage Server Extensions and other web technologies. FrontPage will restrict features used in the site to those supported on the targeted systems.

Restricting the web features means missing out on some effects, but will increase your potential audience.

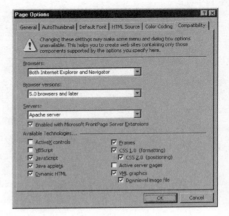

FrontPage webs

A FrontPage web is like any website that consists of a home page plus the associated web pages, graphics, documents, multimedia, and other files that it references. The FrontPage website also contains files that support the FrontPage-specific functions that allow the web to be opened, copied, edited, and administered in FrontPage. The website is created in FrontPage and stored directly on a web server or on the PC hard disk, for use on an Intranet or for later transfer to a web server. The web is stored in a folder or directory. There can be other folders nested within the main folder. The top level is known as the root or parent.

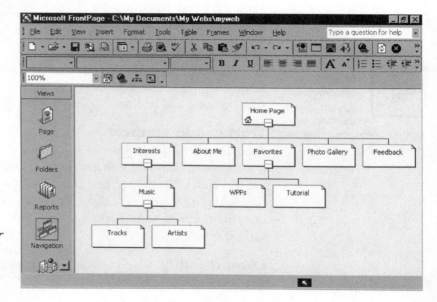

These subfolders of the root web may themselves be complete FrontPage webs. They are known as subwebs, and can have independent administration, authoring and browsing permissions. The subwebs can be used to organise the web into separate sections for different departments or different groups of visitors. Searches and hyperlinks can be limited to the subweb.

For example, you could create a business web for all users, and include a private subweb for employees and another subweb for existing customers. Each subweb could be given the authorities and permissions appropriate to the intended type of user.

Building your website

FrontPage 2002 is designed to handle all the tasks, with assistance from your browser and FTP (File Transfer Protocol) program.

There are a number of stages involved in creating your website. The exact process will vary, depending on the level of complexity in your requirements, and you may need to iterate through some of the stages a number of times, until you achieve the effect you want. However, the basic stages are as follows:

1.   Defining the requirements

Decide exactly what purpose you have in mind when you establish your website. This may be as simple as "gaining experience with the Internet", or you may have specific aims related to your hobbies or business. Whatever the objectives, you should identify your aims and your goals before you start establishing the website.

2.   Designing the website

The website will be a series of interconnecting web pages, plus graphics, documents and other files and components. Choose one of the FrontPage templates to get started.

See also Chapter 12 for links to various style guides for websites, web pages and HTML code.

3.   Creating the components

Build the web pages, collect data, prepare graphics, add links and put everything together to complete the site. Use your browser to preview the results.

4.   Publishing the web

Transfer the components to the web server or LAN server that will host your website, and check that everything fits together the way it should, without, for example, relying on items that exist on your own hard disk. Access the site from a different PC, and try out the scenarios that your visitors will face, so that you can ensure that their visits will be effective.

You can publish updates of any size to your website. However, for major changes, you'd do better to repeat the whole process and build a replacement website.

5.   Maintaining the web

You must keep the information on the website up to date, respond appropriately to the feedback that you receive, and resolve and eliminate any problems or issues that arise.

FrontPage helps you carry out all these tasks. You'll also find lots of help on the Internet in the form of user group, software supplier and standards organisation sites. The World Wide Web itself also provides a multitude of examples of what can be done, and you can see for yourself its impact on visitors.

FrontPage views

In FrontPage 2002, all the design and build tasks are carried out in the one application, with different views for the different stages and activities.

The vertical bar at the left of the FrontPage application window is the Views bar and contains the buttons that switch to different ways of looking at the information in your website.

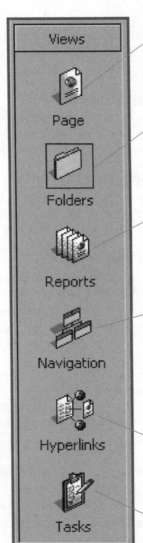

Page view is the view you use for creating, editing, and previewing web pages. It displays web pages as they will appear in a web browser.

Folders view shows how the content of the web is organized, in the same style as Windows Explorer. You can create, delete, copy, and move folders in this view.

Reports view allows you to analyse the contents of your web and calculate the total size of the files, show which files are not linked to any other files, identify slow or out of date pages, and group files by task or assignee.

Navigation view is used to create, display, print, and change the navigation structure of a web. It includes a folder-like view, from which you can drag and drop pages into your site structure.

Hyperlinks view shows the status of the hyperlinks in your web, and includes both internal and external hyperlinks. It indicates graphically those hyperlinks that have been verified and those that are broken.

Tasks view maintains a list of the tasks that are required to complete or maintain the website.

Installing FrontPage 2002

You can add FrontPage 2002 to any PC with Windows 95, Windows 98, Windows NT, Windows 2000, Windows ME or XP. The usual way of installing FrontPage 2002 is as part of the Office XP installation. You won't have to select it specifically, since it is a part of the default setup.

To install Office XP:

If you have disabled AutoRun, open the CD-ROM and double-click Setup.exe in the root folder.

1 Insert the Office XP program CD and the Windows Installer program starts up automatically.

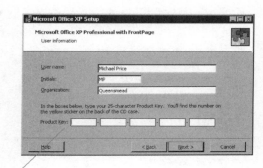

Note that FrontPage includes a set of files used to help build web pages during the tutorial. See page 25.

2 Add your personal details and enter the CD-key for validation.

3 Click to accept the terms and conditions.

You follow similar steps to install the stand-alone FrontPage 2002 product from its own CD. It still uses the Windows Installer but has just the one application.

4 Press Install Now for the default Office XP setup, which includes FrontPage. Select Custom to make changes to the install procedure.

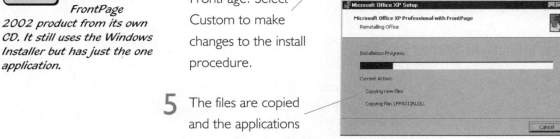

5 The files are copied and the applications are configured.

AutoRun does not run Setup if it finds that Office is already installed.

If you left FrontPage out of your initial Office installation, or if you need to reinstall it for any reason, you can start up Windows Installer in maintenance mode.

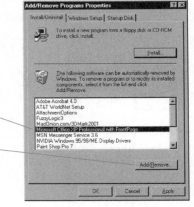

1 Insert the Office CD, open the Control Panel, run Add/Remove Programs and select the Office XP entry from the list.

Maintenance mode provides options to remove Office completely, modify the selection of features, or repair the installation by replacing any invalid files.

2 Click Add/Remove to list or change the installed items.

3 Select FrontPage and click the [+] to expand the list of components. Click the disk icon to choose how to install the components.

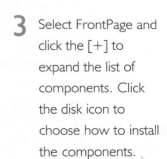

As with all the Office XP programs, you will need your setup CDs close to hand (or a copy available on a server) until you have exercised all the features that you want.

4 Click the Update button and FrontPage components will be installed on the Start menu and the initial files copied.

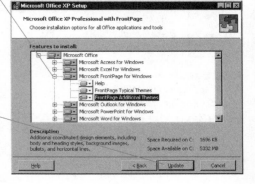

When Windows Installer completes, the selected components will be installed ready for use, or set up ready for transfer on first use, as requested.

Using FrontPage 2002

This provides an introduction to FrontPage by stepping through the creation of a simple website. It uses image and text files supplied with FrontPage, so you can repeat the steps on your own PC.

Covers

Chapter Two

Starting out

As with all of the Office XP applications, a FrontPage shortcut is added to the Start menu during install.

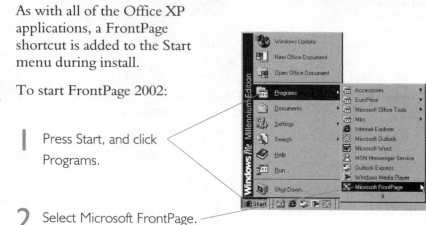

Whenever you run FrontPage, it validates the files and will refresh any that have errors.

To start FrontPage 2002:

1 Press Start, and click Programs.

2 Select Microsoft FrontPage.

By default, FrontPage will open the latest website you've worked on, the next time it starts up. You can change this option if you wish (see page 38).

This displays the main FrontPage window, showing the toolbar and View bar, but with a blank contents screen if this is the first time you've started FrontPage.

Parts of FrontPage 2002:

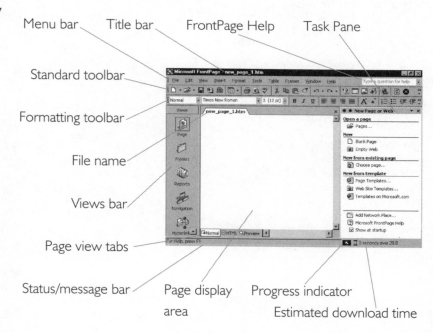

Menu bar Title bar FrontPage Help Task Pane

Standard toolbar

Formatting toolbar

File name

Views bar

Page view tabs

Status/message bar Page display area Progress indicator Estimated download time

The FrontPage tutorial

Microsoft has created an introductory tutorial for FrontPage 2002, but this isn't included on the product CD. Instead, you must visit the download area of the Office website. The current location for the tutorial is at the URL:

http://office.microsoft.com/downloads/2002/fpt2002.aspx

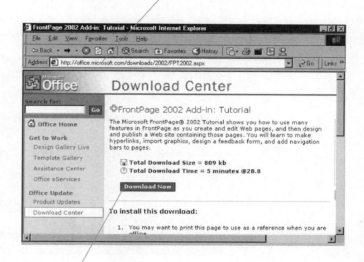

Click Download Now to store FPT2002.exe on your hard disk. Execute the program to extract the contents into a folder named FPTutor2002.

The tutorial is in the form of a Word document that guides you through the process of building a website based on a fictional sporting goods store. Using this as the starting point, you can try out some of the various techniques for creating web pages, publishing your web and making enhancements to improve the presentation.

Creating your first website

The steps involved, discussed on page 19, are to define the purpose, design the web, create the pages, publish and maintain the website.

The easiest way to find out about FrontPage is to go right ahead and create a website. This will introduce you to the style of working that it offers, and show you some of the components and procedures that it supports. You can then examine these in more detail.

The following sections describe how to create and publish a website which provides information about a fictional sporting goods store called Championzone. The online tutorial also builds a Championzone website, though the sequence of activities and the resulting web pages are different. It may be worth reviewing the Tutorial site to compare the effects.

The purpose of the website is to tell your visitors about the sporting goods store called Championzone. The site will contain merchandise information, an online photo gallery, and a list of links to other sites:

Draw a sketch showing the main pages and files or documents to give a pictorial image of the website you have in mind.

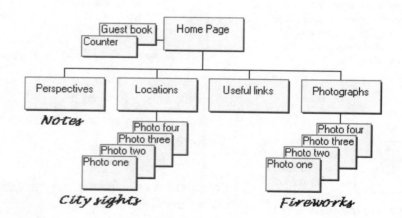

The website will keep a count of the number of visitors, and will capture any comments that they care to leave.

Creating or modifying the website off-line, on your hard disk also means that visitors to your site won't see your work in progress, until it is ready.

You will begin by generating the structure and building the web pages on your hard disk, so you won't need to connect to the Internet until you are ready to publish the site. When that is done, anyone on the Internet can view your pages. However, you can still make changes to the information, adding or removing elements, or inserting new pages whenever you wish, and visitors will see the latest version.

...cont'd

You could start by creating the pages, but it is better to set up the outline structure first. This allows FrontPage to spell check and validate hyperlinks across the site, and maintain dynamic navigation links.

FrontPage will create a website as a unit, with all the information needed to manage the site for you. You should choose one of the website templates to start with, then add pages and links to modify or extend the structure.

To create a FrontPage website:

1 If the Task Pane is not displayed, select File, New, Page or Web.

If a web opens when you start up FrontPage, click Close Web before starting operations on your new web.

2 Under New From Template, select the option Web Site Templates to display the list.

3 Select the One Page web template and then press Tab and specify the location for your new web – for example: C:\My Documents\My Webs\. Add the name Championzone and then click OK.

This creates a new website with a home page which is given the default name Index.htm, so that it will be automatically displayed when visitors enter the URL for your site.

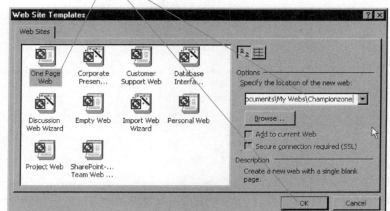

Website structure

If the Folder list does not display, click the Toggle Pane button on the standard toolbar:

I The Folder list shows the home page Index.htm. Press the Navigation button on the Views bar to show the structure.

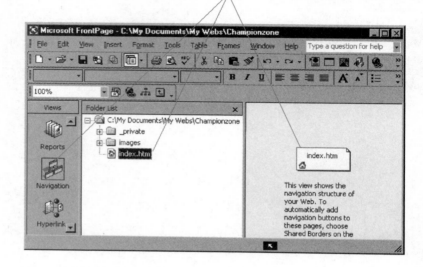

Even though you start with a single page web, you can add more pages and change the structure as desired.

2 Select the home page and press the New Page button, and FrontPage creates New Page 1.

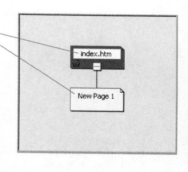

3 Press New Page three more times to bring the total number of new pages to four. Each will be directly below the selected home page:

You can also click Ctrl+N, or right-click the parent page and select New, Page. The new page is just a placeholder until you edit it or import an existing page to add content.

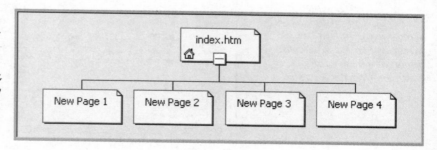

Page titles and names

Every page in the website will have a title and also a file name, which can be different.

The new pages added below the home page are not immediately given file names, so you can re-title the pages and set the file name.

1 With the home page selected, press Tab to switch to the next page in the structure, with the page title ready to edit.

2 Type *About Us* as the title and press Tab again.

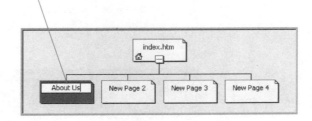

You can change the title of a page by right-clicking it in Navigation view and selecting Rename.

3 Type *Products*, then *Photo Gallery* and then *Links*, pressing Tab after each title.

Internet standards require URLs and file names with plain ASCII characters and no blanks, so that all visitors can follow URLs, without relying on a particular type of PC, operating system or browser. When naming the pages, FrontPage changes the title to lower case and replaces blanks with underscores.

4 Right-click a clear area and select Apply Changes. The files for the new pages are created, using titles as file names.

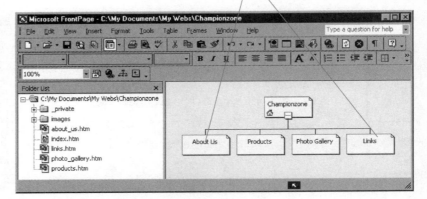

Building the home page

Provide enough on your home page to motivate visitors to stay to view more pages. Think also what encourages repeat visits and recommendations.

Start with the Home page, which is the most important page on the website. It is the default page, the first page that your visitors will see, and it contains the links to the other pages in your website. To add content to the home page:

1 Double-click the home page in Navigation view, or double-click Index.htm in the folder list, to open the file in Page view.

2 Type the title *Championzone!* for your website and then press Enter to start a paragraph.

The asterisk next to the file name indicates that there are changes to the file. Click the Save button, or select File, Save to write the changes to disk.

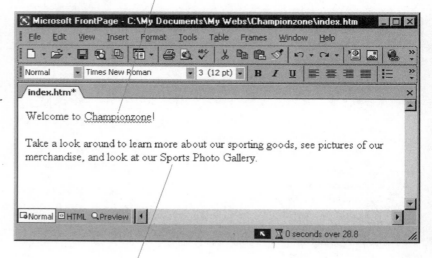

3 Type the introductory message *Take a look around to learn more about our sporting goods, see pictures of our merchandise, and look at our Sports Photo Gallery.* Then press Enter.

Press the Spelling button on the toolbar to spell check the current page (see pages 80–81 for more information):

4 Right-click any underlined words to correct typing or spelling errors, or to add new entries to the custom dictionary.

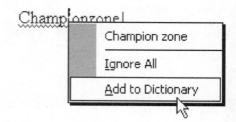

The picture that you add to your web page could be a scanned photograph, a drawing or a PC image file or bitmap.

Now add a picture showing the Championzone logo. To insert the picture:

1 Press Ctrl+Home, then select Insert, Picture, and From File.

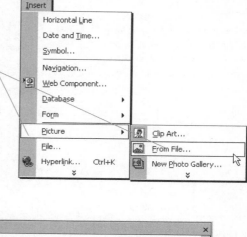

The keys Ctrl+Home put the cursor at the top left margin of the current page.

2 Locate Czlogo.gif in folder FPTutor2002, click the file icon and press Insert.

The picture is added to the page at the cursor location. Press Enter to create a new line.

3 Save the current page. FrontPage makes sure that a copy of the image file is added to the set of files for the website, to ensure that you can still display the picture when the website is published.

The graphics should be saved in the Images folder for the website. Click Change Folder, or drag and drop the image files later, using the Folder List.

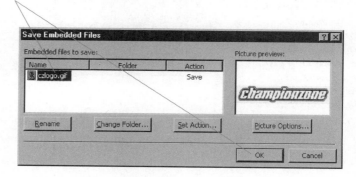

Adding a link

A hyperlink is a pointer to another page or file on the World Wide Web or on an Intranet. Here we attach a hyperlink to a graphic. See page 53–4 for examples of text hyperlinks.

You can make a picture, word or phrase clickable, so that it switches to another web page or a different position on the page.

1 Press Ctrl+End, then select Insert, Picture, From File. Find the file Frontpage.gif in folder FPTutor2002, click the icon and press Insert.

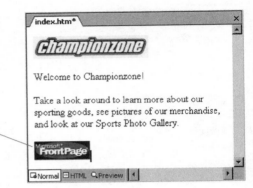

This file is a picture button to indicate that your site is based on FrontPage 2002. You can make it a hyperlink that points to the Microsoft FrontPage website.

2 Click the picture, and the file handles display to show it is selected.

3 Press the Hyperlink button on the Standard toolbar, to display the Insert Hyperlink box.

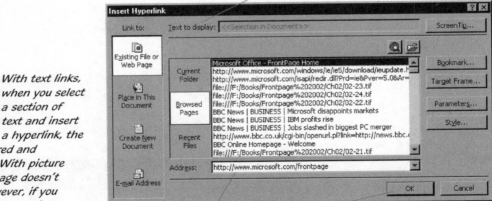

With text links, when you select a section of text and insert a hyperlink, the text is coloured and underlined. With picture links, the image doesn't change. However, if you move the mouse pointer over the graphic, you'll see the URL on the status bar.

4 Find the URL from previously browsed pages or by browsing the Internet, or type in the URL for the FrontPage website – at www.microsoft.com/frontpage – and press OK.

Arranging the items

You can select one or more text and graphics items from the page, and apply changes to layout and orientation.

To centre all the text and graphics items on the page:

1 Select Edit from the Menu bar and choose Select All. Press the Centre button. Click anywhere on the page to deselect all.

The Centre button on the Formatting toolbar centres both text and image items across the width of the page.

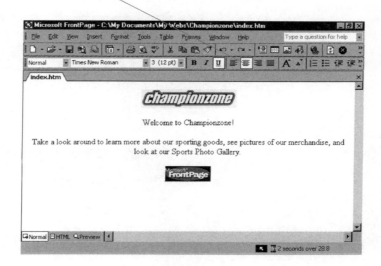

The text and graphics will remain centred across the display, even if you change the screen resolution or the window size.

2 Resize the window and the text and graphics are realigned to maintain the centralised setup.

3 Click the Save button, or select File, Save to make the changes permanent.

Always try your pages at different screen resolutions, to see what your website visitors would get if they had a different resolution than your normal setup.

Viewing the page

You create and edit your web pages in Page view which shows text and images as they will appear, but without animation effects. From this view, you can also see the HTML tags that define the page contents.

1 Select View from the menu bar and click Reveal Tags.

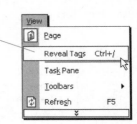

2 Graphical symbols indicate the position of start and end tags for HTML statements.

You can view the HTML tags in a graphical form, so you can see where the tags are placed on the page.

3 Move the mouse pointer over any of the tags to see the details of the tag displayed in a ScreenTip.

Reveal Tags is a toggle, so the setting reverses each time you select it.

4 Select View, Reveal Tags again to turn off the display.

5 Click the HTML tab at the bottom of the page to show the actual coding statements.

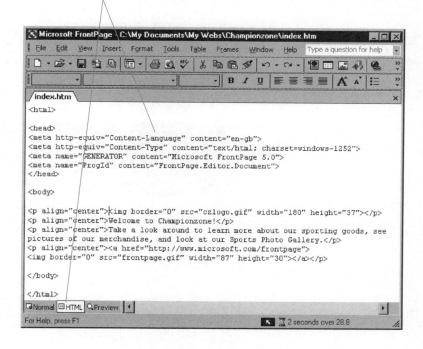

6 To view or change the way FrontPage generates HTML code, click Tools, Page Options, and then click the HTML Source tab.

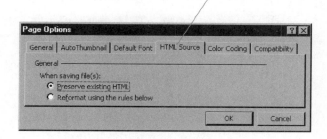

7 Click the Normal tab at the bottom of the page to return to the formatted view of the text and graphics.

Previewing the page

If you use Microsoft Internet Explorer on your PC, you can preview the page as it will appear when it has been published to the website.

To see the page in its final form:

1 In Page view, click the Preview tab at the foot of the display area. Animation effects for text and graphics will be enabled.

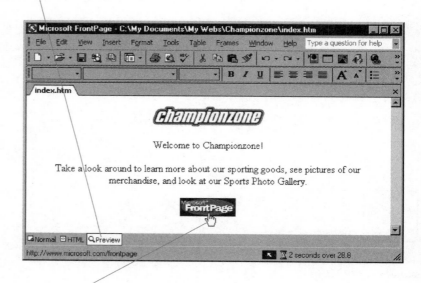

2 Hyperlinks will become live, and will navigate appropriately (though you must be online to access websites).

3 Press the Normal tab to end this preview.

Note that, as long as you are connected to the Internet, you can navigate the hyperlinks even in Normal view. Just hold down the Ctrl key as you click the link, as the screen tip indicates.

You can also view the page using your browser directly. This is necessary if you are using special effects, such as graphical themes (see pages 63–64), or if you are using a different browser than Internet Explorer. First however, you may want to check the web page title (see page 29) since this will be on the browser title bar.

To review or change the page title:

You can also change the title by right-clicking the page and selecting Page Properties.

4 Select File, Save As to view the title. Press Change title to make revisions.

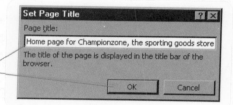

5 Enter a descriptive title for the page, click OK, and click Yes to save.

By default, the title will be based on the first line of text on the page, in this case "Welcome to Championzone", but you may need a more meaningful, descriptive title, since it will be used by Internet search engines.

6 Select File, Preview in Browser, choose which browser (if you have more than one) and the page will be displayed in a new window. Note the page title in the browser title bar.

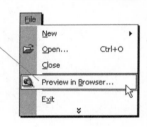

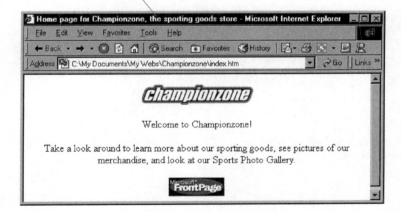

Ending and restarting

When you have finished with FrontPage for the time being, you can terminate the application without explicitly closing the web pages that are currently open.

You are prompted to save any changes or new embedded files.

You do not have to save the web as such. It is actually a folder, with the set of web pages, files and subfolders which contain all the data for the web.

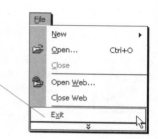

Select File, Exit. All open pages will be closed and the application will end.

FrontPage will remember the web name, and will reopen that web next time you start the application

Choose the Recent Webs item from the File menu, to select the name of the website you want to work on next.

To start working on a different website, select File, Open Web. A second copy of FrontPage is launched, (unless you first chose File, Close Web to terminate the existing session).

If you'd rather that FrontPage doesn't remember, select Tools, Options and click General. Clear the option to Open last Web automatically when FrontPage starts.

If you could be working on a different website each time you start FrontPage, you may not want it to open the previous website every time you restart.

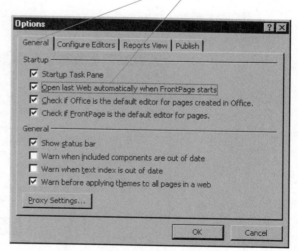

Adding to your web

Continue to build the sample web, completing the remaining pages and showing how to insert text and pictures, check that the pages will download effectively, and create and validate hyperlinks.

Covers

Chapter Three

Inserting plain text

The text that describes the Championzone store has already been created, so you can build your website without having to type in all the information.

To add the contents of a text file to the About Us page:

1 Start FrontPage, open the Championzone web and press the Navigation button on the Views bar to show the pages.

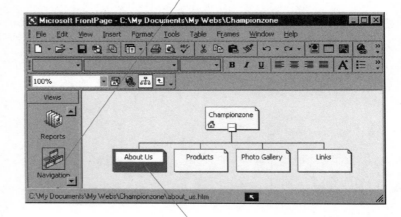

You can also open web pages from the folders list, or using the File, Open command.

2 Double-click the About Us page to open it as a blank sheet in Page view.

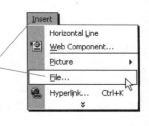

3 Select Insert from the Menu bar and click File. Switch to the FPTutor2002 folder, select the About text file, and click Open to select the contents.

If there are many files in the folder, set the file type to .txt, and then only text files will display.

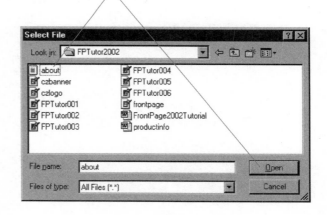

Since the file is plain text, not a Word document or HTML format, you must say how the text should be handled.

4 Choose Normal paragraphs (or Normal paragraphs with line breaks to preserve line ends) and click OK.

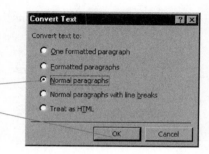

5 The contents of the text file are inserted into the page.

It looks very plain, but don't format the text at this stage. You should apply the themes and any across-the-site formatting before you consider adjusting the layout of individual pages.

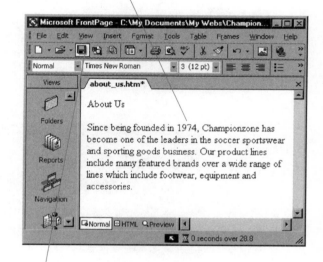

The first time you use a particular file type, you may need the Office or FrontPage CD to complete the installation, since the conversion routines are not installed until they are actually needed.

6 Press the Save button on the toolbar (or select File, Save) to capture the text.

As well as text files, you can insert contents from data files of various formats, including HTML, Lotus, Excel, Windows Write, Word for Windows, WordPerfect and Works. You can even select an option to recover (i.e. extract) text from files of any type.

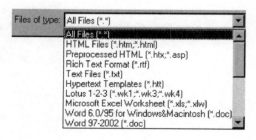

Adding formatted text

There's more text, this time in rich text format, which describes the sporting products, also available from the Tutorial folder.

The Products page will tell site visitors the sporting goods sold by Championzone. On this page, you will also insert several pictures and align them so that the page layout is preserved at different screen resolutions.

1 Open the Championzone website, and then open the initially blank Products web page.

2 Select Insert, File from the menu bar. Locate the FPTutor2002 folder and select the Productinfo.rtf file.

Since the text in this file is already formatted, FrontPage will convert it into HTML form, without requiring instructions. You'll find a page title, some paragraphs of text and a simple list of product names.

Although rtf files have some formatting they may not have the style you want, so you can make changes once the text is inserted.

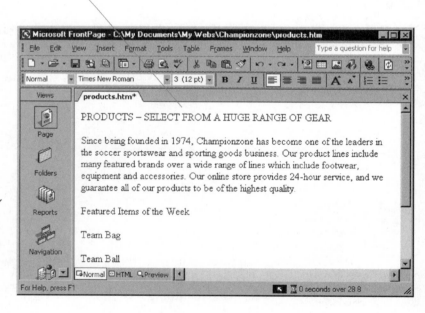

3 Select File, and Save, or press the Save button, to record the addition that has been made to this web page.

To convert the simple list into a bulleted list:

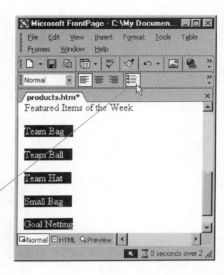

4 Find the list of products on the page. It starts with Team Bag and ends with Goal Netting.

The actual style of bullet will be defined when you select the theme for your website. See pages 63–64.

5 Highlight the list, and press the Bullets button.

6 The selected text is displayed with bullets.

FrontPage supports all the usual word processing formats. To see a list of the functions available:

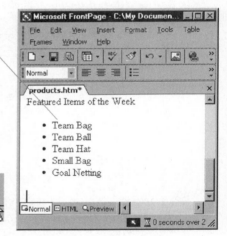

Re step 9 – the following word processing formats are available:

7 Click the down arrow at the end of the Formatting toolbar.

8 This displays the option to add or remove buttons.

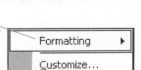

9 Pause the mouse pointer over this command, then select Formatting, to display the list of the formatting buttons with names and keyboard shortcuts.

Adding files to your web

When you insert pictures and text files in a website, FrontPage makes the initial assumption that the files are already part of the site, so it is best to add the files en bloc ahead of time.

To add files to the current website:

When you import a file, a copy is added to your web, and the original stays in the source folder.

You can import files from your hard disk, from a LAN file server, or from the Internet, from a web server.

1 Press the Folders button on the Views bar to switch to Folders view, and open the Images folder which is used to store graphics.

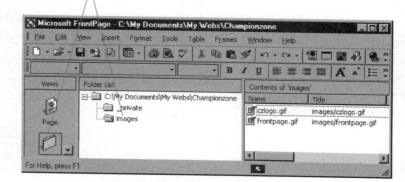

Set the file type to GIF and JPEG, select the first name, press Shift and select the last name, to select all the files. Press Ctrl and click to deselect the files already imported (czlogo and frontpage). Release the Ctrl key.

2 Select File, Import and then press the Add File button.

3 Select the required graphics files from FPTutor2002.

4 Click Open to have the selected files added to the Import list for review and revision.

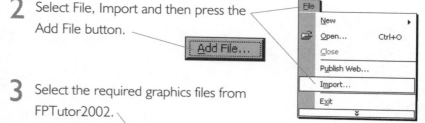

5 Select a file and press Remove, to cancel a selection. Press Add File, Add Folder or From Web to define any other items required.

To quickly import a file or a selection of files to the current web, drag them into the Folder List from Windows Explorer.

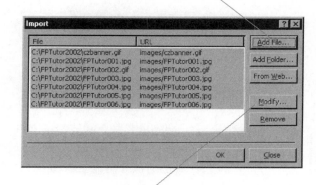

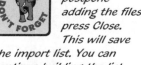

If you want to postpone adding the files, press Close. This will save the import list. You can continue building the list and importing the files later by reselecting File, Import.

6 Select the file and click Modify, to change the destination file name or folder by typing a URL relative to the root of the current web.

7 Click OK to import the selected files, and store them in the target folder in the website.

If you reference files that are on your local hard disk or network drive, they will not be accessible to visitors to your site when you publish the web.

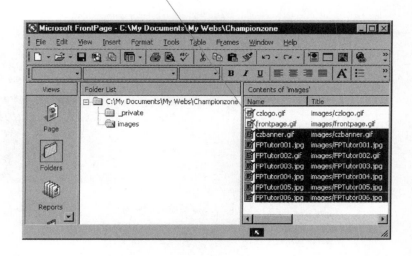

This procedure helps ensure that all the items needed for your web are stored in its folders ready to be published to the Internet.

Wrapping images

Having copied the image files to the website folders, the pictures can now be placed in the web page.

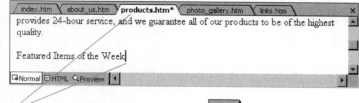

1 Open the Products page and click the cursor just after the heading, to establish the insertion point, then select Insert, Picture, From File.

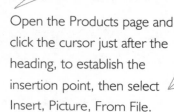

2 Open the Images folder for the Championzone web. Select the picture file FPTutor001, and click Insert to add it to the Products page. Then click on the picture to select it.

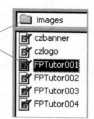

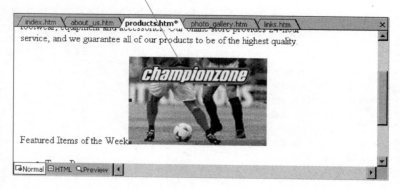

3 Select Format from the menu bar and click Position to display the position panel.

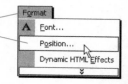

...cont'd

You can also position a picture at the right by selecting it and
clicking the Align Right button on the formatting toolbar:

4 Choose Wrapping style Right and press OK.

This will align the picture with the right margin of the page and the text will flow around it on the left side of the image.

5 Repeat steps 1–4, this time choosing an insertion point at the end of the main heading. Select the picture FPTutor002 and again select the wrapping style Right.

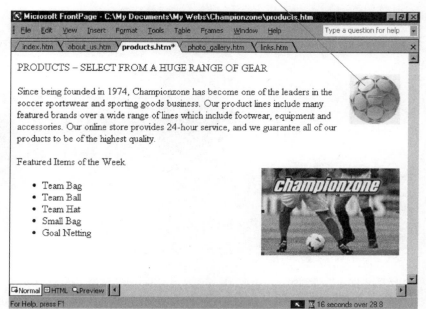

By positioning pictures in the margins, your page layout will be preserved
when the page is viewed at a different resolution and size than the default that you use for creating the website.

A page of photographs

One type of web page that is very popular with web builders is the page of photographs. FrontPage provides Photo Gallery functions for exactly this purpose.

1 Open the Photo Gallery page and type the heading and the text.

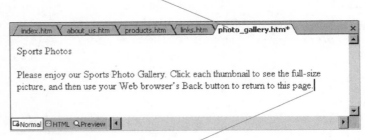

2 Click at the end of the text, click Insert Picture From File from the Standard toolbar, and select four pictures FPTutor003–006 from the Images folder. Press Insert to add them to the page.

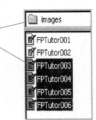

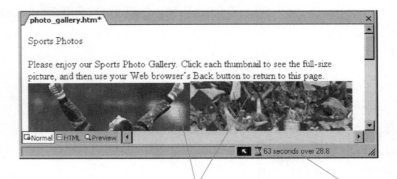

3 The pictures are inserted below the text. Note that the estimated time for downloading this page is 63 seconds at 28.8 Kbps.

The page as created, with the four photographs inserted, will not be appreciated by most visitors, because of the long download time before they can decide if they are interested in the contents.

Unless your visitor has a very high speed connection, the download times with full pictures will be far too long.

The status bar displays an estimated time for the page to download over the Internet, assuming a speed is 28.8 Kbps.

To check the timing for other speeds:

4 Click the Hourglass icon on the status bar, select a different line speed, and note the new time.

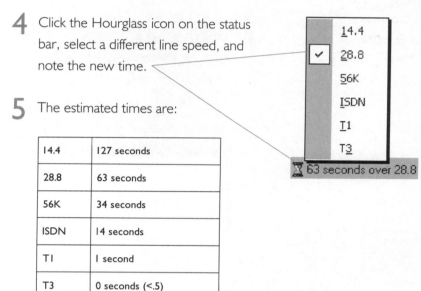

5 The estimated times are:

14.4	127 seconds
28.8	63 seconds
56K	34 seconds
ISDN	14 seconds
T1	1 second
T3	0 seconds (<.5)

These are best case estimates assuming that there are no delays anywhere over the links between your PC and the website server.

With these times, many visitors may lose interest and press Stop on their browsers before seeing what is there. If you want visitors to be pleased with your site, make sure that delays are minimised and they know when they will be transferring larger amounts of data.

You should replace the pictures with smaller thumbnail versions. Then the page will appear quickly, with enough of a preview to urge a closer look. By selecting an individual thumbnail, the visitor explicitly requests the full picture, and only one picture at a time need be downloaded. FrontPage will generate the smaller version for each picture. However, it is usually easier to use the Photo Gallery to do the layout. First however, remove the test photos.

See pages 50–51 to create a Photo Gallery feature.

6 To reverse the photographs, click the arrow next to the Undo button

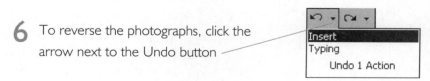

Photo Gallery

FrontPage includes the Photo Gallery with predefined layouts for photographs and other images.

You can add a Photo Gallery component to the web page, to manage collection of photographs or other image files. You can also add captions and descriptions to the images, reorder the images, change the image sizes, and switch layouts.

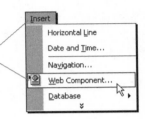

1 Press Enter twice, after the text, to create space for the photos. Then select Insert, Web Component.

2 Select Photo Gallery from the left, and Horizontal Layout from the right.

FrontPage doesn't alter the original picture files. It makes a copy of each picture, resizes and resamples it to reduce the display resolution, and associates a hyperlink to the original picture file.

The thumbnail images are stored in a Photo Gallery folder added to the website.

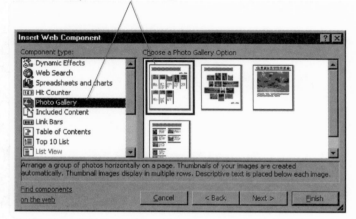

3 From the Properties panel, click Add, Pictures from Files.

4 Select the four pictures FPTutor003–006 from the Images folder, as before. This time they will be stored separately from the web page.

The Photo Gallery Properties panel will be redisplayed, listing the selected image files.

To make changes and adjustments to an existing Photo Gallery, right-click the pictures and select Photo Gallery Properties from the quick menu.

Select a layout

Add images

Edit image

Remove image

Adjust size of thumbnail

Sort images

Set default

Set font

Add image caption

Add image description

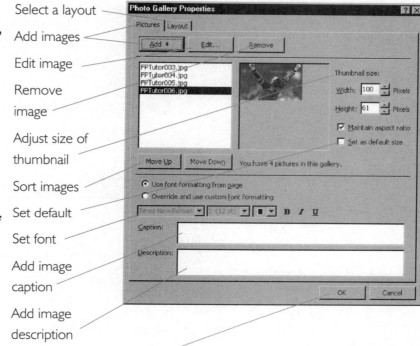

You can use the same font as the rest of the page, or set up custom font definitions for the Photo Gallery text.

5 Press OK to record the changes to the page and save the embedded thumbnail pictures:

In Normal view, press Ctrl and click the thumbnail image, to see the full image. In Preview you just click the thumbnail – no need to press Ctrl.

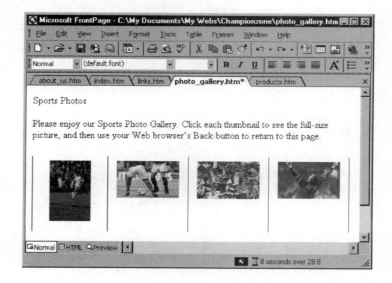

Links page

To set up the Links page for Championzone:

1 Open the web page Links.htm, type *Links to Sports Sites* as the first line, and press Enter.

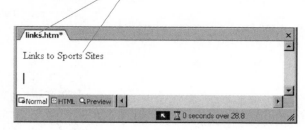

2 Click anywhere in the text and select Format, Dynamic HTML Effects, to display the DHTML Effects toolbar.

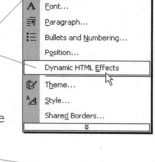

3 Choose On, Page load and Apply, Hop then click the Close button to register the effect.

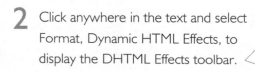

4 Press the Preview tab, or select Preview in Browser from the Standard toolbar, to see the dynamic HTML effect in action.

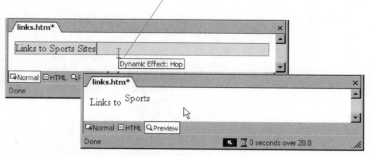

Creating text hyperlinks

You can turn a selected item of text into an active link to a page or a file in your website, on your local file system, on a web server, or on another site on the Internet.

To enter the ® Registered sign, select Insert, Symbol, click the character, then press Insert and Close.

I Press the Down arrow, type *MSN® Sports* and press Enter. Then highlight the text and select Insert, Hyperlink.

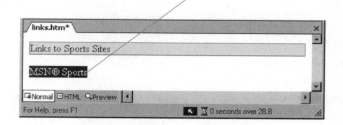

2 In the URL box, type *www.msn.co.uk/sports/* for the UK sports page, then click OK. FrontPage automatically puts the http:// prefix.

You can associate a URL with a graphic to create a picture button (for an example, see page 32).

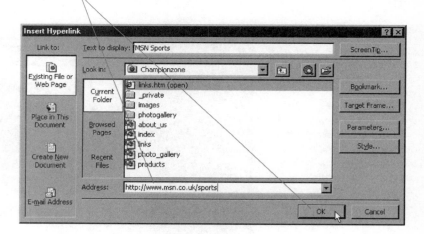

3 Press the Down-arrow to deselect the text. Note that the text is underlined and coloured blue to denote a hyperlink.

When you press Ctrl and click this link, or just click if the page is displayed in a browser, you will display the MSN sports page.

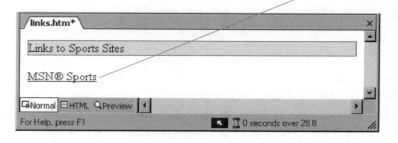

Automatic and verified hyperlinks

To become an automatic hyperlink, your text must start with www. The actual URL in this case is:

http://sports.yahoo.com

but your browser will locate the correct page if you type:

www.sports.yahoo.com

1 On a new line enter the text *www.sports.yahoo.com*. This is automatically made into a hyperlink.

2 Highlight the text and type replacement text *Yahoo! Sports*. The associated URL is not changed.

The best approach is to use your web browser to validate the URLs, though you must be connected to the Internet in order to check out website addresses.

You can also copy URL shortcuts from your Favorites list, or from an existing hyperlink on a web page, by right-clicking and selecting Copy Shortcut, then pasting into the URL box or straight onto the web page.

3 On a new line, type *The Football Association*, highlight the text and press Hyperlink, then Browse the Web. In your Browser type *www.the-fa.org*.

Add the links that you find helpful and want to tell your visitors about. When you have finished entering links, press the Save button on the toolbar to record the changes to your web page.

4 Press Alt+Tab to switch back to FrontPage Insert Hyperlink and click OK to associate the now verified URL with the text you placed on the web page.

Enhancing the web

Continue working with the Championzone web, adding formatting and navigation bars and graphical themes. Preview and test the website and prepare it for publication on the World Wide Web.

Covers

Chapter Four

Formatting headings

Choose fonts and formats that make your website look interesting, but try to be consistent.

When you have created the pages for your website, you can apply font and text style changes to the contents. It is helpful to tackle the pages as a group, so you can easily compare the pages and provide similar effects.

To open all the pages in the web and apply styles to the paragraph headings:

FrontPage always opens a web with a new, empty page ready for use. You can ignore this since it goes away when you open one of your existing pages.

I   Select Folder List, highlight all of the web pages, right-click the section and click Open.

2   Click the Page tab for the home page Index.htm

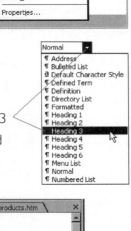

3   Click in the heading text, and select Heading 3 from the Style list. The text is made bold, and the size is increased.

Heading styles are universal HTML standards, and range from level 1 (the largest size) to level 6 (the smallest).

4   Click the Page tab for the About Us web page, click in the heading text and apply the Heading 4 style. The text is again made bold, but the size is unchanged.

To be more accurate (and make it less tedious) you can use the Format Painter to copy an existing format to other pieces of text.

5 Reselect the About Us heading and double-click the Format Painter button on the toolbar. The cursor is given a Painter symbol.

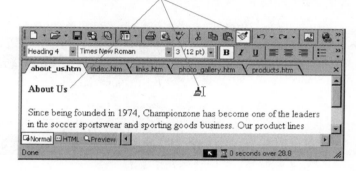

If you double-click the Format Painter, it remains selected until you click the button again. If you single-click, the Format Painter is deselected after first use.

6 Select the Products page and click the heading to apply the format. Repeat the process for the Photo Gallery page heading.

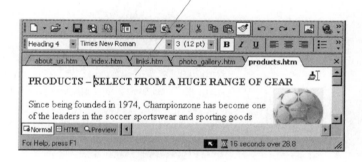

You should not use Format Painter for text that has other formats such as DHTML effects, since it would replace all the formatting and hence switch off the extra formatting.

7 Click the Format Painter to clear the selection, open the Links page, click the heading and apply the Heading 4 format.

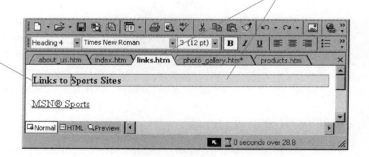

Connecting pages

Creating pages is only the first stage. You must link your web pages together to make them into a true website.

Start FrontPage and open the Championzone web, and select View, Navigation to show the five web pages created so far:

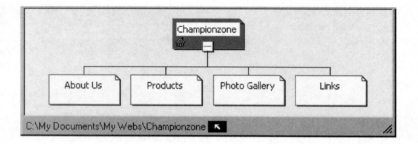

These pages have hyperlinks to image files and links to other websites, but as yet there are no links between the pages within the site.

There are several ways you could add links between the pages:

Manual hyperlinks

You can manually create hyperlinks on the home page to the other four pages, and also put links on those pages, i.e. back to the home page. These links will allow your visitors to navigate around your website. This method gives you the most control over the connections between the pages, but is the most effort also.

You must define shared borders for your web pages, to store the Navigation bars (see pages 60–61).

Navigation bars

FrontPage can create, manage, and automatically update hyperlinks that connect the pages in your web. You can make changes and additions to the web without having to explicitly update the links.

Frames

Frames divide the browser window into different areas, each of which can display a different page. These are known as Frames pages. One of the frames can be used to contain a list of hyperlinks to the pages in the web. This requires more manual intervention when pages change, but the same Contents frame can be used on all the pages, so the amount of updating is minimised.

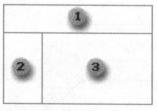

❶ The Banner frame

❷ The Contents frame

❸ The Main frame

The FrontPage Banner and Contents template provides a layout that includes a Contents frames page. See page 138 for details.

This manual approach lets you see what is involved in connecting pages, but you'd have to revise the links whenever you add, remove or rename any pages.

Press Ctrl+End, and drag & drop each of the four file names in turn, to add them onto the index page as hyperlinks.

To complete the link, you'd need to add a link to Index.htm at the foot of each of the other pages.

2 Open Index.htm, press Ctrl+End, and drag & drop the page file names from the folder list to the foot of the page.

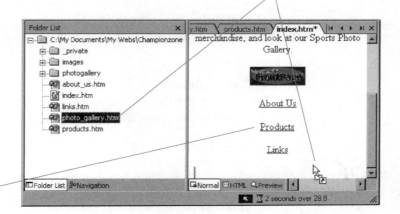

3 Select View, Hyperlinks (or press Hyperlinks on the Views bar) to see the links from the Index.htm page.

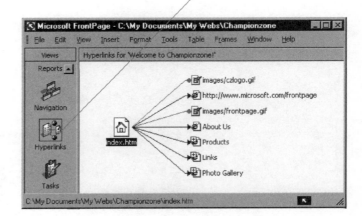

FrontPage can manage all these links for you, without you having to explicitly create the connections, so that your website is automatically updated when you add or remove pages.

4 To let FrontPage make and manage the links for you, click the down-arrow next to the Undo button, and select the last four 'Drops', or close the Index.htm page without saving the changes.

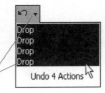

Shared borders

FrontPage uses shared borders and navigation bars to manage the hyperlinks that provide the connections between the pages of your website.

A shared border is a region that is common to some or all of the pages in your web. It may be along any edge of the page (top, bottom or either side). You use shared borders to position the same content (for example logo, copyright notice or contact details) on multiple pages, to save changing each page individually. It also means that you only have to modify content in one place to update all pages.

You can set shared borders defaults for the web as a whole, and apply individual changes to the settings for particular pages, for example turning off a shared border on certain pages.

Shared borders can be used to hold page banners. These display the page title or other text. You also use shared borders to hold the FrontPage navigation bars.

You add shared borders, page banners and navigation bars to webs created through Navigation view only.

To create shared borders across your website:

1 Open the web in Navigation view and select Format, Shared Borders.

2 Select the All pages option.

3 Select Top, and Include navigation buttons.

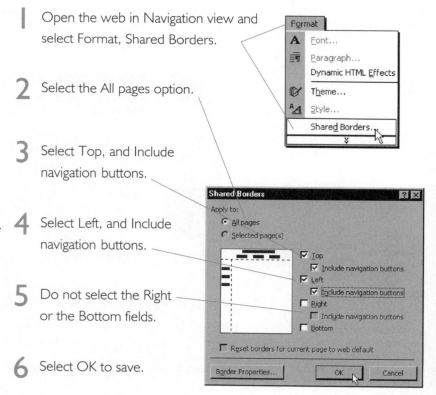

FrontPage creates shared borders and default navigation bars for all the pages in the website.

4 Select Left, and Include navigation buttons.

5 Do not select the Right or the Bottom fields.

6 Select OK to save.

Instead of creating links, let FrontPage create and maintain them through the navigation bars in the shared borders.

With shared borders enabled, the Home page has a page banner and an empty links bar at the top. On the left is a bar with hyperlinks to the lower level pages.

7 From Navigation view, double-click the home page.

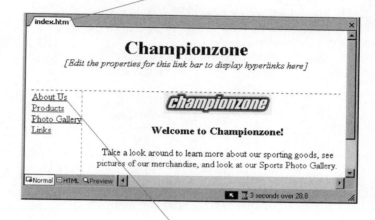

8 Hold down Ctrl and click About Us to display the page.

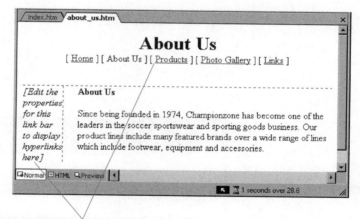

The About Us page (like the other second level pages) has the navigation bar on the top border, but no links in the left border.

By default, the top border shows pages at the same level and the left border shows pages below the current pages. No bar appears when there are no qualifying pages.

For the Championzone website (see page 30), the default settings will be changed, to show a horizontal link bar on the home page, and vertical navigation bars on the other pages.

Customising link bars

Since the changes apply to all pages, you can adjust the properties from any of the web pages.

1 Double-click the text message on the top border for the About Us web page, to open the Properties for the Top bar.

2 Click Child level, clear the check marks for Home and Parent Pages, and click OK.

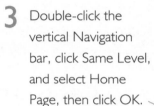

3 Double-click the vertical Navigation bar, click Same Level, and select Home Page, then click OK.

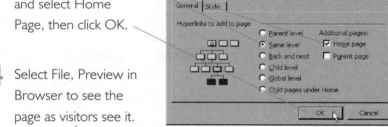

Use Preview in Browser rather than the basic Preview tab, to see the bars in their final form.

4 Select File, Preview in Browser to see the page as visitors see it.

The Top border shows the page banner only, since there are no lower level pages. The left navigation bar shows all five site pages and will include any new pages at one level below Home.

Graphical themes

Despite all the effort so far, the web pages are still quite plain. It takes colour and graphics to liven them up and make them into a real website.

You are saved the detailed design job, since FrontPage has more than 50 professionally designed themes to apply to your website. These specify bullets, fonts, pictures and buttons, and are applied to pages, page banners and navigation bars, to produce an attractive and consistent appearance.

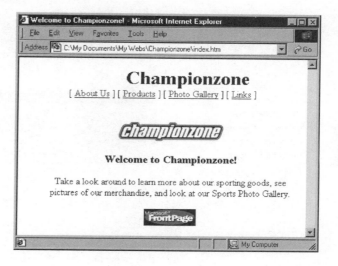

1 Select Format, Theme, and click on any name to explore the options.

2 Select the theme Blends, and choose to apply the theme to all the web pages.

Try the options to see how they affect particular themes. You may need to apply the theme and preview it in the browser to get the complete impact.

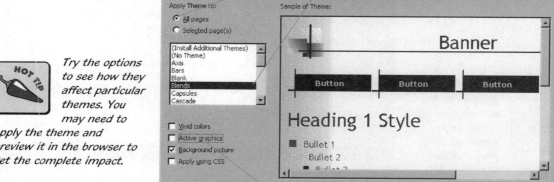

3 Clear the box for Active graphics and click OK to apply the theme.

The first time you apply a theme to the website, FrontPage displays a message to warn you that applying the theme will overwrite some of the manual formatting you may have made.

The theme will be applied to all the pages and borders in your web.

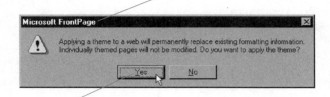

4 Reply Yes to override manual format changes, to display the home page in Normal view with the theme applied.

5 Save the page and select File, Preview in Browser to see how the pages will display on the Internet.

By default, the vertical bars are displayed as plain text, so they still look the same after you apply a theme. However, you can change the default after a theme is applied.

All the pages in the web will inherit this theme. However, you will see that the vertical navigation (link) bar in the left border still shows plain text hyperlinks.

Graphical navigation

Active graphics to enable page banner animations and navigation bar rollover effects, To see a theme's active graphics effects, apply the theme and then display the page in the Preview tab, or click the Preview in Browser command on the File menu.

I Open About Us and note the plain text hyperlinks. Double-click the left link bar

2 Select Style, click Use Page's Theme, and then click OK.

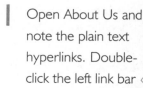

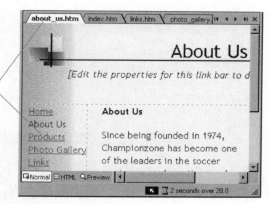

You should scroll to the top of the list of styles to find the entry that says Use Page's Theme.

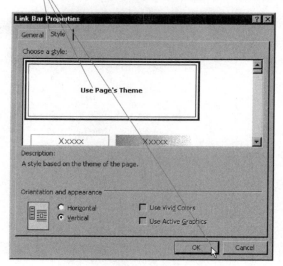

The horizontal link bar already uses the settings from the theme, so you don't need to change that bar's properties.

3 Click anywhere on the page to deselect the navigation bar.

FrontPage changes the format for the left link bar to use the graphical buttons included with the theme.

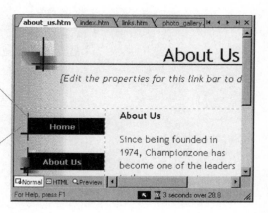

Customising the theme

The banner for the web pages shows the page name in large text. You can modify the theme to create a more graphic banner.

1 Open the website and the Home page, select Format, Theme, and select Blends, the default theme for this web.

2 Click Modify, and then Graphics from the set of option buttons added to the panel.

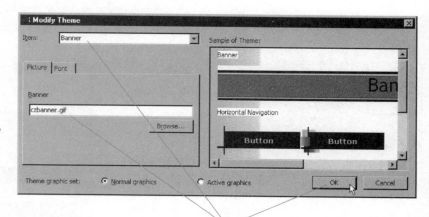

3 Select Banner from the Item list. Select czbanner.gif and press OK.

The new banner file replaces the banner from the original theme.

4 Click Yes to save the changes you've made to the theme.

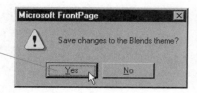

The supplied themes are marked as read-only, so you must save an existing theme under a new name.

5 The Blends theme is read-only, so you must provide a name such as Championzone for the modified theme.

6 Click OK to apply the new theme to the website.

The new theme is applied to all the pages in the web. The effects show up immediately, in the Normal view.

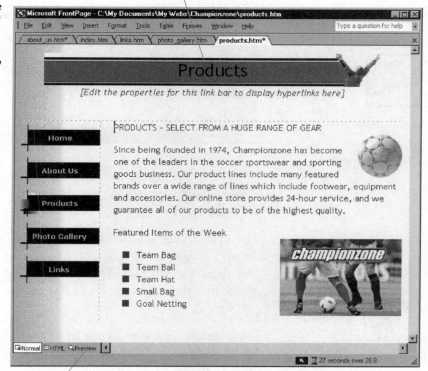

7 To see the page without placeholder text or formatting marks, press the Preview button, or select File, View in Browser.

Arranging files and folders

You arrange the files and folders in your website using the Folders view. With this you can change the locations of files without worrying about invalidating hyperlinks or losing access to banners, buttons or navigation bars.

To view the contents of the web:

Open the web and press the Folders button on the Views bar (or select View, Folders). Click [+] to expand folders, [-] to collapse.

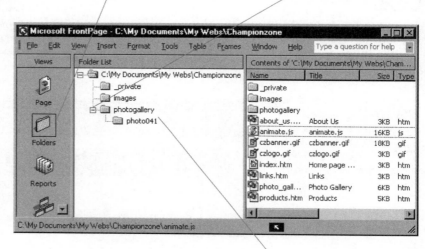

Click once to sort in ascending order, and click again to sort in descending order.

Don't use Windows Explorer or other file managers to rearrange the contents of your web – it would break the hyperlinks.

By default, FrontPage provides a folder for 'images'. If you create a Photo Gallery, FrontPage also generates a folder structure to hold the thumbnail images.

The main folder should normally contain the HTML (.htm or .html) files for web pages. You might have saved embedded images files there also, and DHTML may have added some JavaScript (.js) applet files there. So you could have a mixture of file types.

It is much easier to maintain the web if you group files together. For example, you should put all picture files into the Images folder. You should also have folders to contain special purpose files such as audio clips, video clips or applets. You should use Folders view to rearrange the locations of the various types of files, and to create the additional folders you may require.

...cont'd

Hold down the Ctrl key to select sets of files that are not listed in consecutive order.

2 Select the first picture file, hold down the Shift key and select the last picture file.

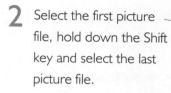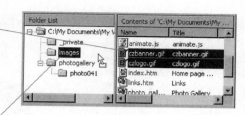

3 Click and hold the left mouse button to drag the selection onto the 'images' folder. Release the button to drop the group of files into the 'images' folder.

FrontPage displays Rename while it moves files since it is updating all the hyperlinks to those files.

4 Right-click the folder within which you want to create the new subfolder.

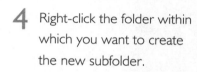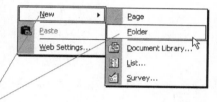

You can create a new page in Folders view, but it won't use shared borders or navigation bars (see page 70).

5 Select New, Folder from the context menu displayed.

6 Drag and drop files from their current location to the new location. For example, move applet files from the main folder to Applets. FrontPage will adjust references as the files are moved.

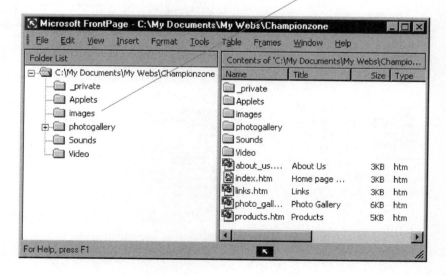

Adding a new page

When you use themes and shared borders for all pages in the web, new pages that you create will inherit the attributes that you have specified. However, you also have to show FrontPage where the page fits in the overall web structure.

1 In the folder list, right-click the target folder and select Blank Page.

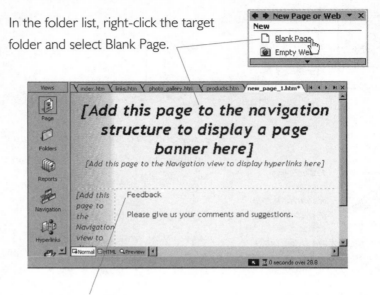

Depending on its level in the structure, the new page may be added to the navigation bars in the shared borders and appear on the other pages.

2 Add the text *Feedback*. Press Enter then add *Please give us your comments and suggestions*. Then select Save. The default name is the first line of text *feedback*.

3 Switch to Navigation view, and drag the new file from the folder list to the appropriate position on the web structure.

This page will be completed with the addition of a feedback form, as described in the next chapter (see page 72).

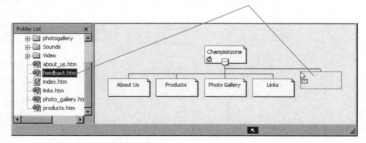

The page will now display the page banner themes etc.

Finalise the web

Add the final items, such as a feedback page. Display reports to check that the web is complete, and confirm that the web is ready for publication on the Internet or the Intranet.

Covers

Chapter Five

Request feedback

With a feedback option on your website, you can gain information as well as distribute it.

The last page added to the web was Feedback. The purpose of this page is to provide a means for visitors to the website to contribute their comments and suggestions. To create a form for responses:

1 Open the Championzone web and the Feedback page, and press Ctrl+End.

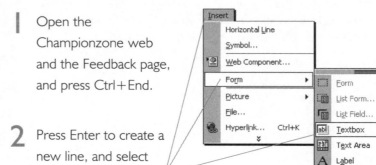

2 Press Enter to create a new line, and select Insert, Form, Textbox.

FrontPage inserts a new form on the current page. The dashed lines indicate the form's boundary. By default, a new form contains Submit and Reset push buttons.

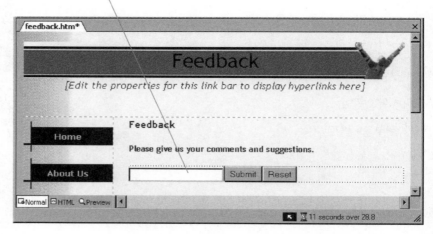

The form makes it easier to collate and interpret feedback, especially if you want the analysis to be automated.

3 With the cursor left of the Submit button, click the Centre button on the toolbar and then press Enter to add an extra line. Press the back-arrow to go to the start of the form.

You can add text boxes, check boxes, menus, radio buttons, pictures and push buttons, to your forms, to make it easy for the visitor to enter useful details.

Holding down Shift while pressing Enter creates a line break. Line breaks are useful for spacing lines of text more closely together than standard paragraph spacing.

The default scrolling text box is very small but can easily be enlarged (see page 74).

To illustrate how to customise forms, you will add several input fields that help visitors supply useful details with the comments.

4 Type *Your Name:* and then press Shift+Enter to create a line break, move the cursor after the text box and press Enter.

5 Type *Your E-mail Address:* and press Shift+Enter. Select Insert, Form, Textbox as in step 2, and add a data entry box. Then press Enter to add a line.

6 Type *Your Comments:* then press Shift+Enter. Then select Insert, Form, Text Area to insert a scrolling text input field.

This provides a scrollable text box with a default width of 20 characters, and allowance for two lines of text in the viewable area, but you can increase the size if desired (see page 74).

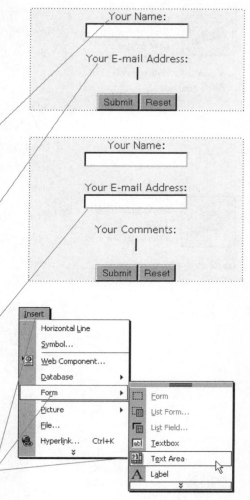

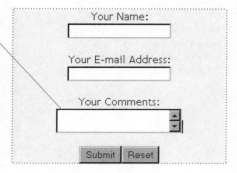

Adjust the form

1 Double-click the scrolling text box to display its Properties.

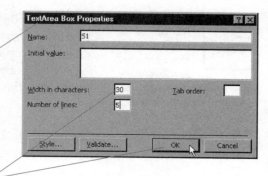

2 Change the width to 30 characters and the number of lines to 5, and press OK.

3 The scrolling text box is enlarged. Press Save to capture the revisions.

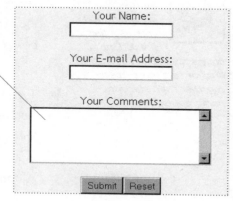

4 Press the Preview in Browser button to view the page in its final form.

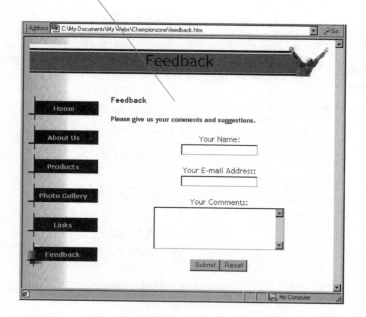

Which browser?

The browser is a key element in your website, since that is how your visitors will access the pages, when you have published the web. It is essential to understand what browsers they may be using.

You don't have to cater for all browsers but you should be aware of the implications of using different browsers, and decide to what extent you can make allowances.

Of course, visitors to your site are not restricted to Windows, so there may be other browsers not available on a Windows platform.

95% of visitors may be expected to use Internet Explorer or Netscape Navigator. Even then, you need to allow for the range from versions 3– 6 currently available for each of these products.

When you view your web pages with your browser, you will see what your visitors will see, as long as they have the same browser as you, or one with support for all the functions that you use. This may be more difficult to achieve than you might think. The Internet.com website keeps track of the types of browsers in use (see http://browserwatch.internet.com/browsers.html) and it lists over a hundred different products, each with their own particular strengths and weaknesses:

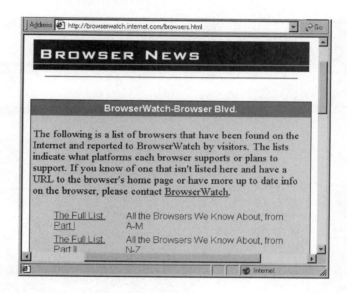

Of course, the majority of users will be using a small subset of these browsers. The Internet.com site for example reports that its visitors used the following browsers:

Microsoft Internet Explorer	89.4%
Netscape Navigator	6.24%
Opera	1.10%
Arachne-xChaos	0.45%
Konqueror	0.36%
Powermarks	0.32%

Add extra browsers

You can't dictate the resources that your visitors will have available, but you can avoid conflicts or at least warn visitors of potential mismatches.

You can install extra browsers on your hard disk, and use them to test your web in addition to your normal browser. You can obtain copies of most browsers from the Internet. For example, for the three main browsers, visit the following websites:

- http://home.netscape.com/computing/download/

- http://www.opera.com/download/

- http://www.microsoft.com/downloads/

To use an extra browser:

The new browser must be already installed on your system, since FrontPage checks the command line.

1. Open a page in your web, select File, Preview in Browser.

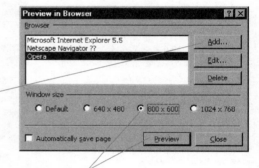

2. Click Add, enter the command line to run the browser, and click OK. Then select the

Your choice of screen size and browser will become the defaults (as used by the Preview in Browser button) until you select different settings.

screen size and browser, and click Preview.

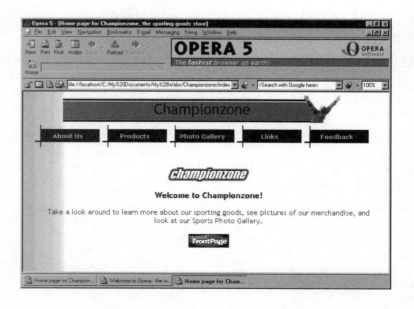

Review the web

View all the pages in your website. Note any items that fail to operate as expected. Repeat the checks with other browsers. If there are browser-based limitations, you can modify the items, or add a suitable caution to the page.

You would switch back to FrontPage to centre the Photo Gallery and delete the blank line above the thumbnail images.

When you make any changes in FrontPage, Save the page, and press Reload or Refresh to see the effect in your browser.

1 Open the Home Page, select File, Preview in Browser and pick the window size you use as your preferred size i.e. 800 x 600.

2 Click on the Navigation bar to change web pages. For example, select Photo Gallery.

3 Observe the layout and note problems. For example, the photo thumbnails could be centred and be moved up higher.

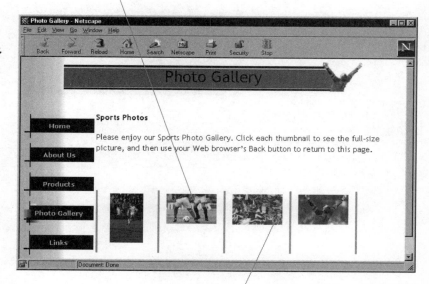

4 Click on a Thumbnail to display a photograph full size.

5 Click the Back button to return to the main Photo Gallery web page.

Modify text

You can make a
change to
selected pages
or all pages in
the website,
but you can only replace text
in parts of the page that can
be edited directly. Text in
page titles must be modified
individually.

You can make global changes to the website if there are terms that
you use on several web pages, and you decide they need adjusting.
To modify a section of text:

1 From any view, select Edit, Replace.
Choose All pages, and enter the current
and new text values.

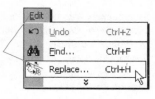

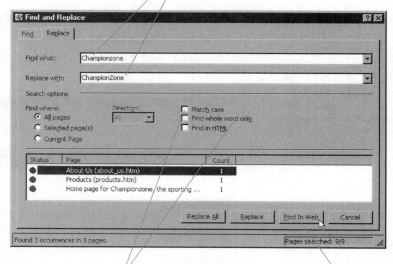

You can skip
individual pages
where you are
sure that
changes to the
text would not be
appropriate.

2 Set Match case or Find whole word only if needed and press Find
In Web. Double-click the first entry to open the relevant page.

3 Apply changes to the
current page. Click
Find Next to skip a
change, or Replace to
change and find next.

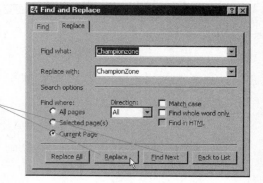

FrontPage guides you through the changes, reminds you to save the changed files and makes sure that you do not leave out a page by mistake.

4 When each page is finished, you are prompted to save and close the current document and move on to apply the changes to the next page.

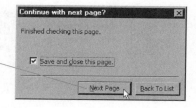

5 When the final page is completed, you are prompted to save and close the last document.

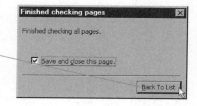

FrontPage 2000 featured an Add Task button which allowed you to add the Replace operations to the Task list. This option is not available in FrontPage 2002.

If the changes definitely apply to all pages, you can complete all the replacement operations in one step.

6 Press Replace All to change all the occurrences immediately. Press Yes to confirm, or press No to cancel the operation.

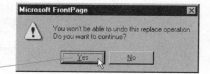

When you use the Replace All function, the report shows which pages have been edited and how many changes have been made.

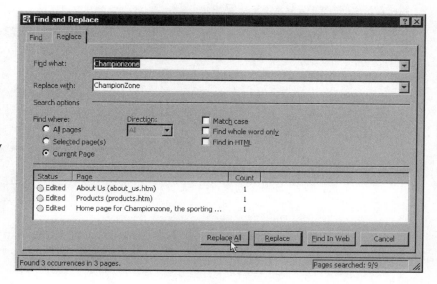

Check spelling

Background spell-checking will identify possible spelling errors with underlines. You can retype the words or use the spell checker to correct them, as you build the individual pages. However, you should also make it a practice to carry out a full spell check of all the web pages, just before you are ready to publish the website.

To check the spelling for the entire site:

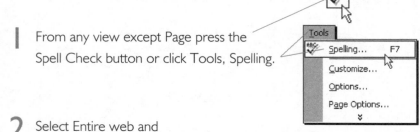

1 From any view except Page press the Spell Check button or click Tools, Spelling.

2 Select Entire web and Add a task for each page with misspellings.

3 Click Start and FrontPage analyses the text and displays the results.

4 Click Cancel to finish with Spelling.

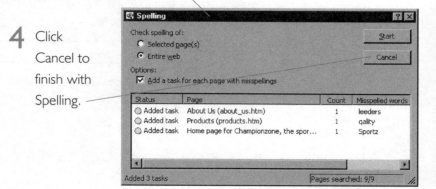

The spell check is completed, and the change instructions have been added to the task list, but spelling corrections will not yet have been applied to the text.

The Tasks mechanism makes it possible for several people to apply checks on a large web, and then have all the tasks completed at one time. This reduces the possibility of multiple concurrent changes that could cause some changes to be lost or overridden.

To display the list of Tasks:

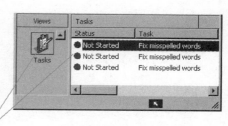

5 Select the Tasks icon on the Views bar, and the Tasks list is displayed, with the details for each task .

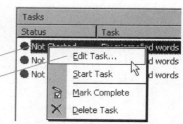

6 Double-click a task on the list, or right-click the task and select Edit Task in the menu.

The details of the selected task are shown. You can change the task name, set the priority, assign it to someone else in your group. Click OK to save changes.

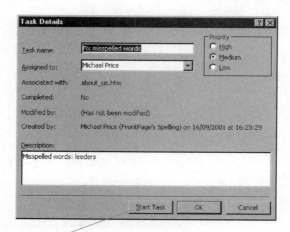

Additions are made to the custom dictionary used by the other Office applications, so you won't have to add special terms for every application separately.

7 Click Start Task, or right-click a task and select Start Task, to open the page.

You can Ignore special terms that are rarely used, Change to one of the dictionary suggestions, Add new terms and names to the dictionary, as well as correcting mistyping and spelling errors.

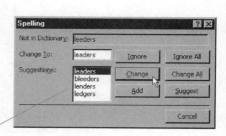

Mark tasks complete

1 Click OK when the spelling corrections for a page are completed.

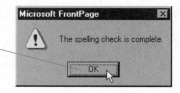

2 Select Save for the page, and you are prompted to mark that task as complete.

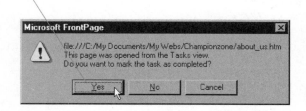

3 If you don't update the status when the associated file is saved, you can right-click the task and select Mark Complete at a later time.

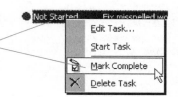

4 Start the next task, and continue until all the tasks have been marked as completed.

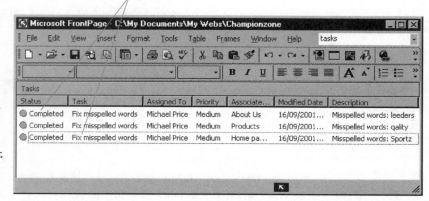

Create new tasks

You can use the Tasks list to record the need for any type of activity. For example, you could assign a research task to an individual in your group, and log the task in the list. When the research report has been produced, mark the task as completed.

You can assign tasks, prioritise them, and link them to a page or any other files in your web. When the tasks are finished, you can mark them as completed, in the Tasks list.

To create a task:

1 Open the web, press the down arrow next to the New button, and select Task.

2 Enter details for the task (e.g. name, performer, priority and description) and then press OK.

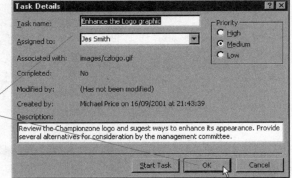

If you create a task in Page view while editing a page, the task is automatically associated with that page. To associate a task with a page or file in another view, select the file, and then create the task. If no pages are open, the task will carry no file association.

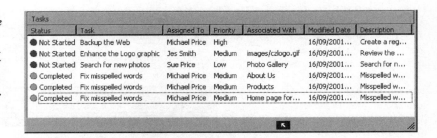

You can choose to hide or display your completed tasks:

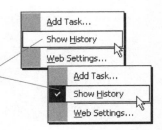

3 Right-click the background in Tasks view and click Show History to toggle the display on or off.

Web reports

FrontPage provides reports to help you identify any problems with your web, before you send the files or the updates to the web server.

The Reports view gives you information about the status and condition of your web, so that you can find and resolve any shortcomings before you publish it. There are over a dozen report categories, but the place to start is the Site Summary.

To display the default report:

1 Open the web and press Reports on the Views bar to display the default report (the Site Summary).

To change or reset the default, you'd select Views, Reports and click the report that you'd like to see displayed when you open the Reports view.

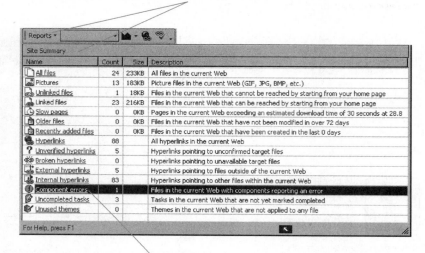

The 'Site Summary' gives you an overview of the website. 'All files' tells you the disk space you will require at the web server. 'Slow pages' warns of any pages that may be a problem during download, and the various hyperlink reports tell you if there are any issues with links.

2 Click the link on a report line to see more details. For example, click Component errors to show the list of files reporting an error.

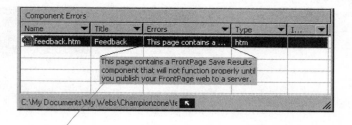

FrontPage reminds you that the response form works only when the web has been published to a server that supports the necessary extensions. This is a warning only.

...cont'd

If you rename or relocate files using the Folders view, the integrity of URLs will be maintained. Using normal Windows commands will invalidate the URL references.

The Broken Hyperlinks report will alert you to any errors in hyperlinks. These could be due to mistyping of URLs, or to changes in file names or locations made after the URL was set up.

For the detailed list of the broken hyperlinks in the web:

Any invalid hyperlinks are displayed. FrontPage will also list the unverified external hyperlinks, and will verify them for you.

3 Click the link to the Broken Hyperlinks report entry. It's worth checking, even when the summary line shows zero errors.

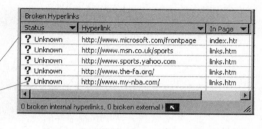

4 Click Yes to verify if you are connected, or click the Verify Hyperlink button on the Reports toolbar at a later time.

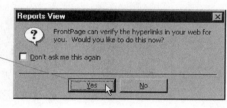

If there are many external hyperlinks in the web, it may take some time to carry out this command, since FrontPage must connect to each external website to verify the hyperlink.

5 FrontPage connects to the Internet to check out the links.

6 Right-click a hyperlink and choose Edit Hyperlink or Edit Page, to correct any errors in hyperlink addresses. You can also select Show all Hyperlinks to see the full list of hyperlinks, both internal and external.

Backup

You can make a backup copy of all the files and folders in the web. However, the preferred way is to publish the web to a folder on your hard disk. This ensures that all necessary files are saved, in the correct structure.

1. Open the web, and press the Publish Web button on the toolbar (or click File, Publish Web).

2. Click Browse and locate the backup folder, then click OK to publish.

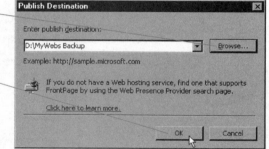

3. If this is the first time you've used this folder, then FrontPage will create a website structure for you.

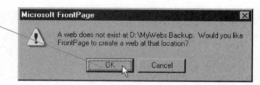

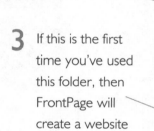

4. Specify Include subwebs and click Publish, and FrontPage transfers the files and folders of your web to the specified destination.

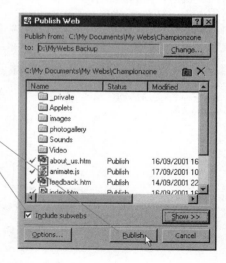

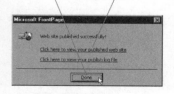

Publishing the web

When you have all the components, and you have checked all the links, you can finally transfer the web to the Internet. The process depends on the type of ISP or WPP you are planning to use.

Covers

Chapter Six

Ways to publish

When you are ready to display your web on the Internet or on your company Intranet, you must publish your web, which means copying all the files and folders in your web to a web server, where visitors can browse. You should already have checked for broken hyperlinks (see page 85), and verified that the pages look the way you expect.

To publish to the Internet, you need an ISP, preferably one offering a web server with FrontPage Server Extensions or Microsoft SharePoint Team Services installed. You also need the web server location, and your user name and password.

SharePoint Team Services from Microsoft is a team website solution included with FrontPage 2002. You use it to create workspaces to manage group activities.

FrontPage Server Extensions

The server extensions are not essential, but they give your web the full FrontPage functionality, such as form handlers, search forms, hit counters, and component features. FrontPage will maintain your files and hyperlinks. Each time you publish the web, FrontPage compares the files on your local computer to the files on the web server. If you move a file in your web on the hard disk, FrontPage will update and correct any hyperlinks to it, and then make the same corrections to the web server files, the next time you publish the web.

You can also edit the web directly on the web server, though in that case the hard disk version will not stay in sync.

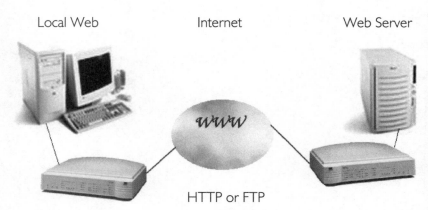

Local Web   Internet   Web Server

www

HTTP or FTP

HTTP or FTP

The server extensions also influence the way you publish the web. If your web server has the extensions, then FrontPage can publish using HTTP (Hypertext Transfer Protocol). Otherwise, your web will be published using FTP (File Transfer Protocol).

ISP and FTP

Don't use the Publish Web button, since this will automatically use the last destination defined, even if that was just for backup to your hard disk (see page 86).

This is the method to use if your ISP does not have explicit support for FrontPage 2002 server extensions.

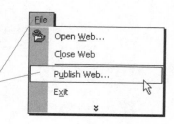

1 Open the web and select File, Publish Web to start the process.

2 Enter the FTP address for the web server providing your web space.

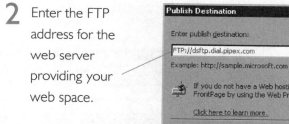

Specify All Pages the first time to replace existing files, and click Publish. There may already be a page called Index.htm at the website, perhaps as a placeholder by your ISP.

3 Enter the account ID or user name and the password, and then click OK.

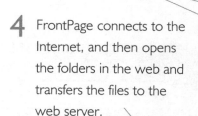

4 FrontPage connects to the Internet, and then opens the folders in the web and transfers the files to the web server.

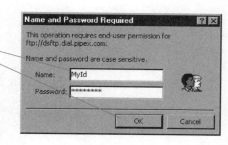

Try asking your ISP (or your network administrator for an Intranet) to install the features. At least they'll then know that there is a demand.

5 FrontPage will detect if the server does not support FrontPage extensions and warns you if any pages need them.

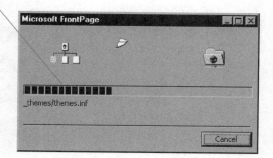

Because you have used FTP to publish the site, FrontPage cannot offer the link. Use the address provided by your ISP to view the website (but not the FTP address). See page 12 for examples of addresses.

6 When all of the files have been transferred, the Website Published message is displayed.

7 Open the browser and enter the URL for the website, and check out the hyperlinks.

You'll find that most functions work as you'd expect, though perhaps with a much slower response, compared to the local web, since everything must be downloaded from the web server.

Click on the Photo Gallery button to switch to the Photo Gallery web page. Click the thumbnails to see the photographs full size on your web server.

Try the form

Dynamic features such as FrontPage forms may appear to work but won't complete properly without the server extensions. See page 98 to see how the form operates when the server extensions are supported.

Various Internet sites offer Guest Book facilities that manage responses for you without requiring special functions on your web server.

Alternatively, you can take advantage of email to get responses.

Re step 2 – you'd need to change the page to use a different method that does not depend on the extensions. For example, insert a MailTo address hyperlink so you can get responses via email:

Feedback
Please give us your comments and suggestions.

Contact the Championzone
Webmaster

I Display the Feedback page. Even without server extensions, your browser will allow you to complete the fields in the form.

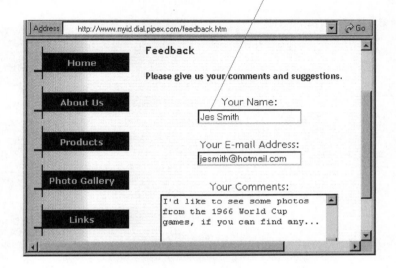

2 However, when you press the Submit button, if there are no server extension to process the form, you get an error message.

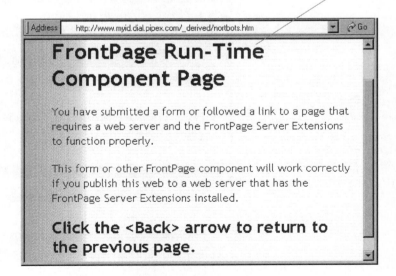

Select a WPP

If you want to find an ISP that offers support for FrontPage–enabled websites, you'll find help at Microsoft's website.

To view lists of Web Presence Providers:

1 Select File, Publish Web and click the Change button. Then select the link to the Web Presence Provider search page.

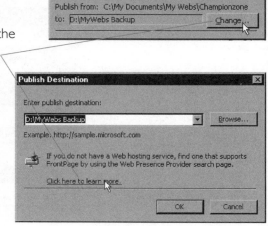

2 The UK web page for providers of Office/FrontPage websites is displayed.

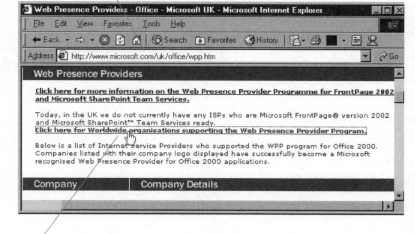

3 There will eventually be a specific link for UK WPPs, but in the meantime click the link for International WPPs, to find a list of ISPs that will support FrontPage 2002 server extensions.

If you do not see a suitable WPP listed here, select the list of WPPs that support FrontPage 2000-based websites. These may already be updated to support the newer versions, even if they are not yet on the Microsoft list.

You can fill in the ISP name, the services required or the location to find other WPPs (USA or Canada) which provide support but have not yet been formally tested.

Use a search engine such as google.co.uk to find UK WPPs.

Alivewww specialise in web hosting and do not provide dial-up support. You can use any Internet Service Provider to give you access to the Internet, and you can manage your Alivewww website from that ISP.

4 Click the link for one of the registered WPPs for FrontPage 2002 and/or SharePoint Team Services to get details of their facilities.

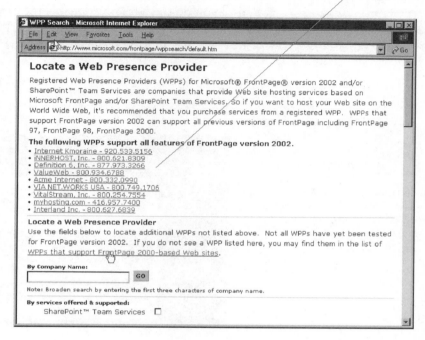

5 Not all available services are listed by Microsoft. For example, Alivewww.co.uk supports the extensions and provides web hosting for up to 250MB of data at charges as low as £1 per month.

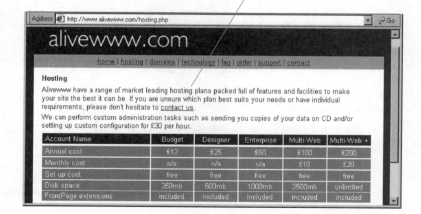

Set up your WPP

FrontPage server extensions allow you to use the publication feature and dynamic page element available in FrontPage.

You can send your web pages and related files to your WPP using FTP as you would for an ISP. However, if your WPP supports the FrontPage server extensions, you can use HTTP for the transfer. Before you do this you must enable the extensions for your website. The details may vary between WPPs but the main steps will be similar. For the Alivewww hosting service:

1 Sign on to the Control Panel for your account and select to use FrontPage server extensions on your website.

The User Control Panel is a web-based administration interface which allows you to control all aspects of your web hosting account, including security, scripts and FrontPage extensions.

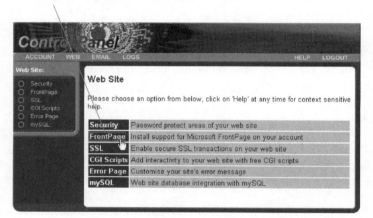

2 Enable your account and choose to install the FrontPage Server Extensions on your website.

Once you have enabled the FrontPage extensions on your website, you will no longer be able to upload your files by FTP. Selecting the option to Uninstall FrontPage Extensions will restore FTP access.

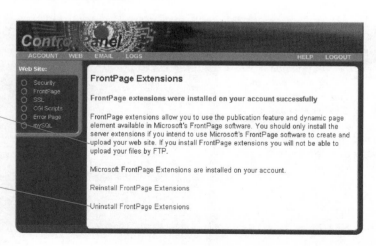

Domain names

See page 12 for more examples of website addressing

options..

The WPP will provide you with an account name that you can use to specify the address for your website. For example, with Alivewww and an account myaccount, you could address your website as: http://myaccount.alivewww.co.uk/

If you want a full domain name such as mydomain.co.uk, so that you can address your website as: http://www.mydomain.co.uk, you need to register the domain name and pay an annual fee. There are many domain registration services, but for the UK, one of the simplest and least expensive is 123-reg.co.uk.

1 Open the http://www.123-reg.co.uk website and open an account. This is provided at no charge.

2 Sign on with your account name and password, and choose to order a domain name. Specify the name you'd like to use.

You will find that many of the usual names are already taken, and you may have to try a number of options before finding a name that is not yet in use. Not all endings need be free for you to use a name, as long as the ending you want is still available.

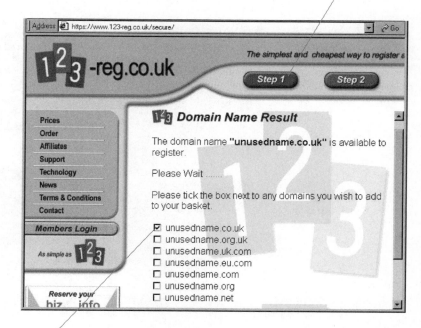

3 Select the ending or endings that you wish to use with your name, and these will be assigned to you. The process may take two or three days to complete and make the URLs addressable.

Publish to your WPP

This is similar to publishing to your ISP, but you use the Internet HTTP protocol rather than the File Transfer Protocol.

FrontPage checks that the extensions are enabled at the target site, then asks you to sign on.

Note that the website is shown with Realm, FrontPage Extensions, which is required in order to publish the web using HTTP.

1 Open the web, select File, Publish Web and press the Change button to set the destination.

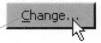

2 Enter the URL address for your new website.

3 Enter the account ID and password for your WPP account, and then click OK.

FrontPage compares the files on the source and the destination, and decides which files should be sent to the website.

4 Show the folders and files at the destination.

Select to include Subwebs.

Change the properties.

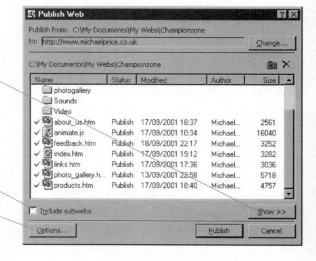

With Options you can choose to send changed files only, comparing the source and destination versions by time stamp or by contents.

5 FrontPage connects to the Internet, and opens the folders in the web to transfer the files to the web server hosting your site.

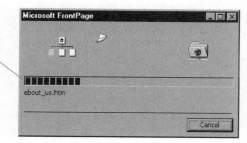

6 Click the URL link on the message, or open your browser and enter the URL, to switch your browser to the website.

The Home page for your web is displayed. When you open the site, all the pages and features of your website should operate just as they did with the ISP setup. However, this time you should be able to use the form on the Feedback page to collect observations left by visitors to the site.

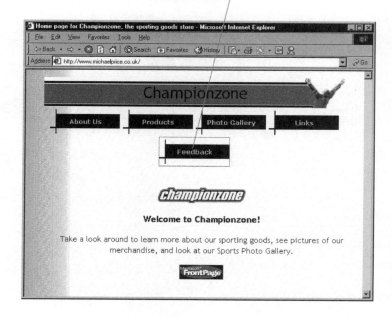

WPP form

If the WPP supports FrontPage extensions, and you have enabled the feature, the dynamic features such as FrontPage forms will now operate correctly.

I Click the Feedback button on any of the pages in your website to display the FrontPage form.

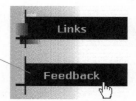

2 Click in the first box and type your name.
Press Tab and enter your email address, press Tab again and put your comments.

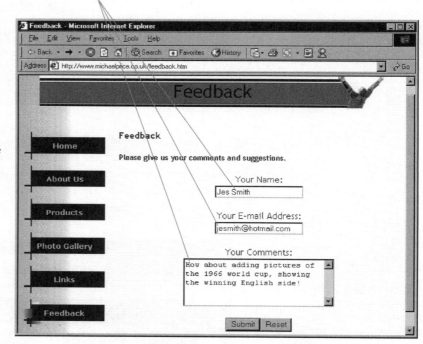

The form contents are written to a file in the website (see page 97 opposite).

3 Remember you can create as long a message as you want, using the scrolling text box.

Your Comments:
the English side! That might
bring back some happy
memories and remind us that
sometimes the impossible does
happen.

4 Press Reset if you want to clear the form and cancel your message, or press Submit to record the message.

By default, FrontPage forms use simple field names such as T1, T2. You can choose meaningful names when you create the form, using form field properties (see page 73).

When you submit the form, the details are written to file, and a confirmation message shows the fields recorded.

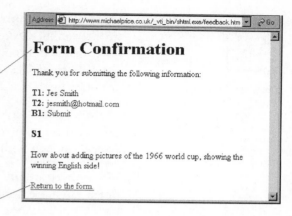

5 Press the Back button or click the link to return to Feedback.

6 On the address bar, replace *feedback.htm* by the folder name *_private*, press Enter and type your account name and password.

Only the website owner or someone with the proper password can access the results file.

7 Right-click the file of forms results, select Save Target As, and save it in the _private folder on the hard disk.

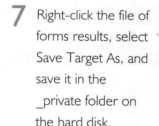

When you save results files to the hard disk copy of your web, you must be careful to avoid republishing the results file and hence overwriting new responses. See page 100.

Open the form_results file to see the comments displayed in a spreadsheet format, one response per row, with the field names used as the column headings:

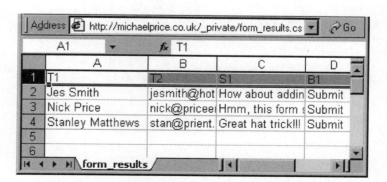

Selective publishing

You may need to restrict publication of some parts, for example while they are still under development.

When you first publish your web, you usually publish all pages. FrontPage then automatically switches to publish only files that have changed. It compares the files in the web on your hard disk to the published files on the web server. Only newer versions of files are published.

FrontPage also looks out for files that have been deleted or relocated on your hard disk copy, and synchronises the files on your local web with the published files on the web server.

When there are incomplete pages that are still under development, or files that are not currently part of the web, you may want to prevent publication of particular files.

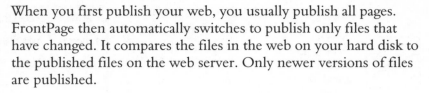

Some files are published only once, e.g. comments, guestbook entries or hit counters, to avoid overwriting collected data.

1 Select View, Reports, Workflow, Publish Status and choose the file or files that you want to protect from update.

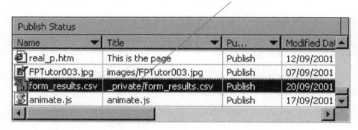

You can right-click the file icon from the Folder List in any view, click Properties on the shortcut menu, and then click the Workgroup tab. However, using the report allows you to select files from multiple folders at the same time.

2 Right-click the selection, choose Properties and then click the Workgroup tab.

3 Click Exclude this file when publishing the rest of the Web. Despite the wording, it can be applied to multiple files in a selection.

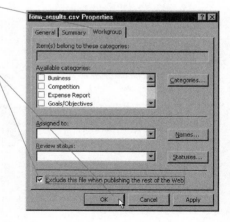

4 To re-enable, select the files and clear the Exclude... box.

Promoting the web

The best design won't help if no-one knows about your web, so you need to add the information that will get your URL added to the search sites, to encourage visitors and references for your website.

Covers

Chapter Seven

Will you be found?

Designing an exciting website and publishing it to a server is really only half of the job. You have to ensure that other Internet users know about your site. Then you will get visitors to enjoy your work, and perhaps some suggestions for improving the site.

There are many ways in which people might find particular websites, for example:

- Follow links provided by their ISP.

- Follow links found on other websites.

- Find a website using a search engine or directory (Google, Yahoo!, Infoseek etc.).

- Click on a banner heading or in a secondary window.

- Find out a URL address by word of mouth.

- See a URL address in a review, advertisement or brochure.

- Receive an email with a website URL address.

Some of these methods apply to the larger business, but many may be equally applicable to the small business or the personal website.

To get started with promoting your website, consider the following options:

- Make use of the facilities offered by your ISP or WPP for raising awareness of your site.

- Tell your family, friends and business associates, with an email announcement.

- Make sure that you are listed by the search sites, with a good description and in the right category.

- Run a small ad or issue a press release to a local newspaper or to a magazine dealing with your particular topic.

Your ISP or WPP

ISPs and WPPs are usually keen to provide links to their account holders' websites. You'd complete a form to give the title, description and category for the website:

Freeserve collects similar details but registers your website at 12 different Internet search engines, as long as you use their ZyWeb design aid. When you are using FrontPage, it's left up to you to register the site.

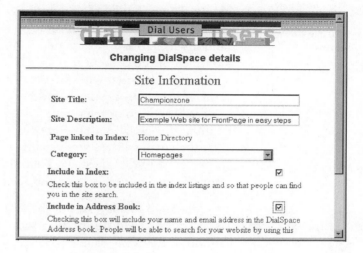

All visitors to the Dial Pipex site (account holders and guests auditing the ISP facilities) are encouraged to visit Dialspace. Their searches will be applied against the details provided through the forms. Take advantage of this to view designs from other users.

Visitors can search all sites in Dialspace, or just a specific category. They can find your Dialspace site even if it is not registered with any Internet search engines.

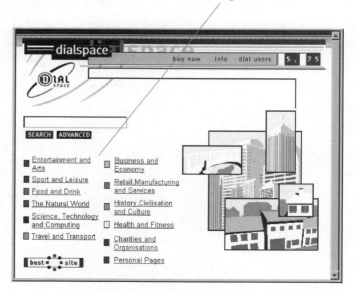

Announcement

1 Send a message with a brief description of your website, and quote the required URL.

Make the announcement text sufficiently detailed to interest and intrigue, but don't include so much of the content that curiosity is satisfied without a visit. If it is appropriate, include an email address or telephone number for queries. Remember that the email address you use for sending the announcement will be attached to that message. Your email program should have a "send using" option, so you can select a suitable email address.

Put the Send to addresses in the Bcc box, to avoid distributing all your contact addresses with the announcement. Don't make the announcement message too personal to the recipients. It should be general purpose enough that your contacts feel able to forward it to their contacts. You can always send separate, personalised notes to introduce the announcement.

2 Add your website URL to your email signature, to act as a reminder to your contacts whenever you send email.

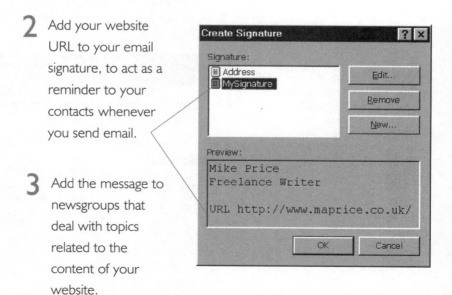

3 Add the message to newsgroups that deal with topics related to the content of your website.

How sites are found

Extend beyond the limits of your immediate circle and appeal to the Internet as a whole.

To find a website, page or other element, you choose a search engine such as AltaVista and enter the details of your query in the form provided. This is the way most people locate websites that may be of interest to them.

1 Select the type of item you want to find – images, audio files, videos, websites or just a general search.

Advanced search options let you state your query more precisely, to minimise the number of inappropriate matches.

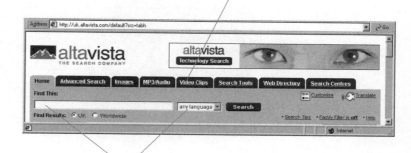

2 Type keywords or phrases defining the item, or enter a question. You can limit responses to a particular language or geography.

3 Click Search and await the results. There may be a long list but better matches are closer to the start of the list.

You want to be sure that searches for topics related to your website will include your URL in their results, near the top. This can only happen if the search engines know about your site.

You should note that there are three types of search site. These are:
- *search engines that use robots*
- *directories that use people*
- *hybrids that are a mixture*

Search sites may rely on being told about URLs, and their staff visit and review the web pages, to decide whether to add the URL, and what categories to use. Others send out web robots that roam around the Internet looking for new or updated web pages. The URL, page title, and selected text from the pages are sent to the search site. Some search sites use both methods.

To increase your chances, you can register your URL with specific search sites, or include meta-variables in your web pages, to feed data to the search robots.

Register your URL

Registering your site with a search engine or directory is free of charge. The procedure for each search site may vary, but the examples of Excite and Snap illustrate the main techniques. To register with Excite:

1 Open the search site at http://www.Excite.com and look for the Submit a Site link towards the bottom of the page.

2 Locate the Add URL link and click to display the registration form:

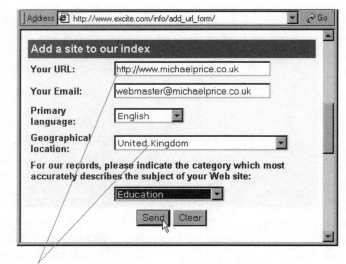

3 Enter the URL for your site, a contact email address, the language and location. Select a category from the list.

When you have finished filling out the form, click the Send button to submit your request. Excite does not guarantee it will be added.

Suggest your site

With directory sites such as Yahoo! you should select one of the predefined categories and subcategories, then click the Suggest a Site link. You can add your URL to Yahoo! for no charge, or use the quicker Yahoo Express, again at a one time charge of $299.

1 Select one of the 14 main categories, and follow the subcategory links to identify the most suitable one for your site.

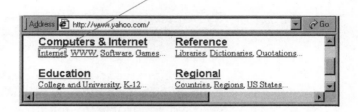

2 With the appropriate category selected, scroll down to the bottom of the page and click the Suggest a Site link.

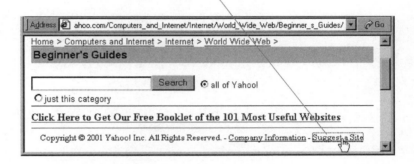

3 Complete the registration form with the title, URL, location, description and any other requested information about your site.

The topic and path will be filled in for you, if you preselect your category.

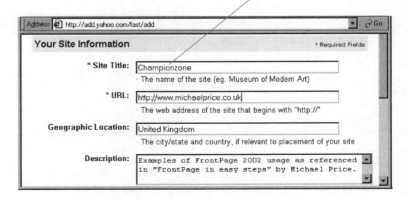

When you submit the request, it is sent to the directory staff for evaluation.

Meta-variable tags

FrontPage allows you to insert data in meta-variables, to hold data for the search sites.

Many search sites will make use of Meta-variables (often called Meta-tags) if available, to collate indexing information. There are two types of Meta-variables:

System variables

<META HTTP-EQUIV="name" CONTENT="content">

These control the action of browsers, and are used to refine the information provided by HTML headers. You normally do not need system variables to index your site.

User variables

<META NAME="name" CONTENT="content">

These specify metadata, information about a document, in name/content pairs providing details. This is particularly valuable when your home page has little or no text, for example when your page is entirely graphic, or with a frames-based site where the index.htm consists of FRAME tags.

Include common misspellings or include different word forms, to increase the chances of your page being selected in a search.

The following user variable types are most applicable for use by the various search sites:

Tags can also be used to exclude a web page from being listed in an Index.

Description	A concise definition of the page contents. Aim to provide about twenty or so words.
Keywords	Terms and synonyms related to the topic of your web page. Choose the words you think that visitors are likely to enter into a search. Separate each word with a comma.
Author	The author or company name. If you want, this could be the target of a search.
Resource-type	Put Document for an HTML page. This is the only tag that you need to put in for indexing purposes.
Distribution	This can be Global, Local or Iu (stands for Internal use). Normally you'd put Global.
Robots	Put Noindex, Nofollow, Noimageindex or Noimageclick to instruct the search site to avoid indexing page or image files, or to avoid following links to private or members-only pages.

To add Meta-tags to your web page:

1 Open the Index.htm page in Page view, select File, Properties and select the Custom tab to create or change meta-tags.

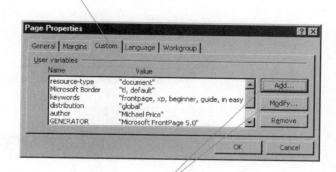

2 Click Add to generate new user variables, or select an existing entry and press Modify to make changes.

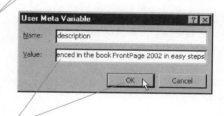

3 Enter the Name and the Value for the variable, and click OK. To view the tags that have been entered, press the HTML button.

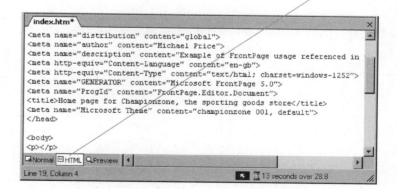

When you have added all the Meta-tags, republish the web page.

Registration services

There are services that will register your website on your behalf, usually for a fee, but some offer free services also.

While it is easy enough to register your website with a few of the main search engines, it can become quite time-consuming if you want wider coverage. The answer is a registration service such as NetPromote which will do most of the work for you.

1 Open the www.netpromote.com website, and select the link labelled Free Submit to register your site URL on 9 search sites.

There's also a free Meta-tags service which will generate the HTML code for the tags that are needed for indexing your site (see page 108).

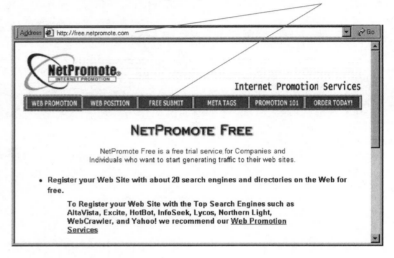

2 Complete the URL and contact data requested, check the search engine selections and click Submit Your Site to begin the process.

The 9 main engines are pre-selected but you can add regional and other search engines.

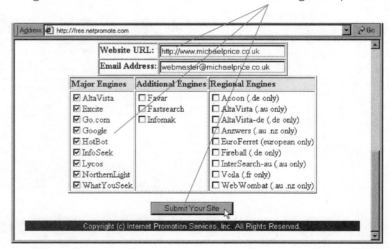

3 NetPromote checks that you have entered valid data, and asks you to confirm the details by pressing Correct! Submit My Site.

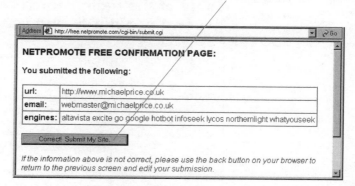

4 NetPromote sends your URL to each of the selected engines, and displays all the replies that it receives back:

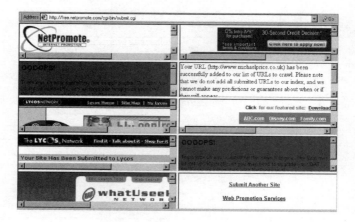

Not all robots honour Meta-tags. Some search sites believe that extracting actual text is more valid.

The search sites do not guarantee to list your URL. Even when you are registered, it may still take several days or weeks for the search site robots to locate your website and collect the additional details from the Meta-tags or from the text within your pages. You may be able to improve your situation by taking advantage of the fee-based registration service which deals with 850 search-related sites, or by using the WebPosition software which shows you how well your site ranks, and how to improve the placement.

Search sites

There are very many different search sites, directories and search engines, for general and special purposes.

There are many search sites available on the Internet, and each may offer regional versions such as UK or Europe.

Some of the main search services (based on general popularity and usage):

Sites may combine but the old name will usually work. For example, if you switch to the old:

www.infoseek.com

you'll automatically be redirected to the replacement site which is:

www.go.com

AOL Search	http://search.aol.com/
AltaVista	http://www.altavista.com/
Ask Jeeves	http://www.askjeeves.com/
Direct Hit	http://www.directhit.com/
Excite	http://www.excite.com/
Fast Search	http://www.allthewebs.com/
Go	http://www.go.com/
Google	http://www.google.com/
GoTo	http://www.goto.com/
HotBot	http://www.hotbot.com/
I Won	http://home.iwon.com/
Inktomi	http://www.inktomi.com/
LookSmart	http://www.looksmart.com/
Lycos	http://www.lycos.com/
MSN Search	http://search.msn.com/
Northern Light	http://www.northernlight.com/
Open Directory	http://dmoz.org/
Planet Search	http://www.planetsearch.com/
RealNames	http://www.realnames.com/
Search.com	http://www.search.com/
WebCrawler	http://www.webcrawler.com/
Yahoo!	http://www.yahoo.com/

You can find details of these and additional search engine sites at the search engine watchers site:

www.searchenginewatchers. com

Checking your website

The contents of your Meta-tags are key to the success of searches for your website, so it is worthwhile checking them before the search engines begin reviewing your site.

To be sure that your website will be properly recognised by the search engines, you can use Northern Web's META Medic to check your website's Keyword and Description META Tags.

I   At the NetPromote website click Promotion101 and locate the Meta Medic link to http://www.promotion101.com/ meta_medic.shtml

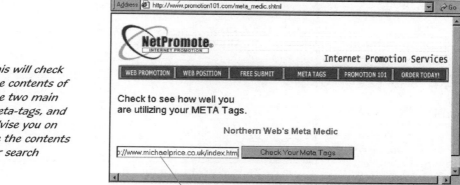

This will check the contents of the two main Meta-tags, and advise you on how to improve the contents to increase your search effectiveness.

2   Enter the full URL for your Index.htm page (or any other page on which you've placed Meta-tags for indexing) to see the analysis:

Meta Medic checks the size of the keyword tag, stripping out commas and spaces. Here it points out that only a small amount of the available space has been used. It recommends a keyword string of between 300 and 500 characters.

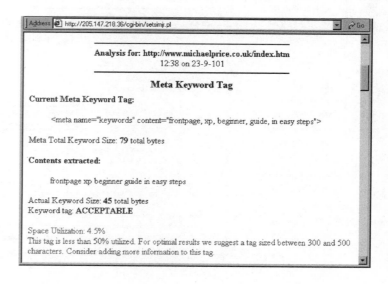

The actual content is extracted from the description tag, and Meta Medic points out that only 40% of the allowed space has been used. It recommends increasing the length of the description.

Meta Medic confirms that both of the Meta-tags are acceptable to those search engines which use them. This entitles you to display the Meta Medic graphic if you wish.

It may be wise to periodically recheck your tags if you do change them.

As the illustration suggests, you should replace the following line of code:

src=http://ww.mysite.com/ mygraphics/metamedic.gif

with the path for your Images folder, for example:

src="images/metamedic. gif"

3 Scroll down the results page to see the comments on the description tag.

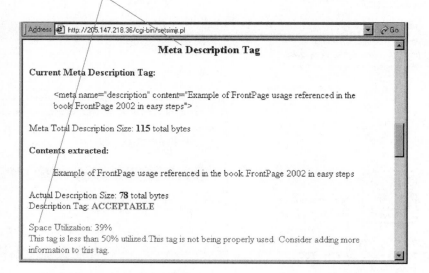

4 Scroll to the bottom of the page to see the summary report. You'll also see a graphic and the HTML code to add it to your page.

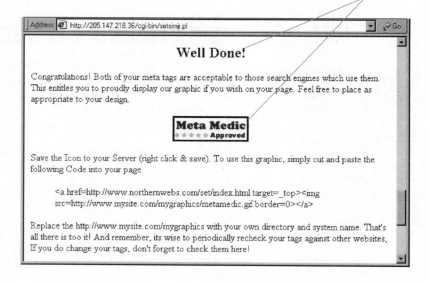

Bells and whistles

When you have published and registered your web, you can start adding features to make sure that visitors find the site worth revisiting and worth recommending. You'll also need to measure the rate of success that you achieve.

Covers

Chapter Eight

Counting on success

To show that the search sites are doing their job, you need some means of checking how many visitors you have had to your site.

A hit counter keeps a tally of the number of visits, and shows the current total on the page. You'd usually put the hit counter on your home page, since this is the normal entry point. Displaying the counter means that both you and your site visitors can see how popular the website has become.

To add a counter:

1 Open the web and the Index.htm page, and position the cursor where the counter should appear.

2 Select Insert, Web Component. Select Hit Counter and choose the type of counter.

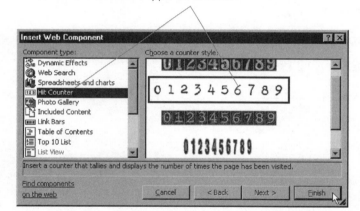

To use the FrontPage web components, you must have a web server that supports FrontPage Server Extensions.

3 Save the page, and republish the web to the web server.

In Page view and the Previews, a placeholder is shown. When the home page is viewed on the web server, however, the counter will be displayed and updated on each visit.

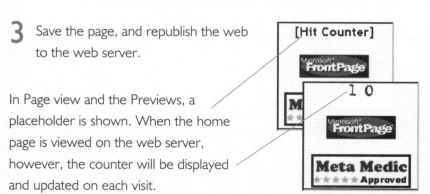

...cont'd

You can reset the counter when you have finished your testing, or if you introduce a new set of topics to the website.

You might wish to add the date when the counter was reset as a comment or as a displayed entry, to put the count into context.

Note that when you reset the counter, the new initial value is saved in a file called Index.htm.cnt. However, the server side code stores the incremental values in a file that's called Index.html.cnt.

If you don't see the new value, you may have to copy and rename the Count file when you reset the counter.

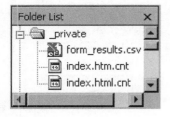

To change counter settings:

4 Open the web, open Index.htm, double-click

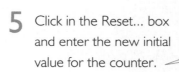

Select a different style.

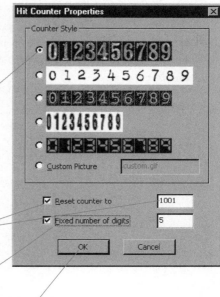

5 Click in the Reset... box and enter the new initial value for the counter.

6 Click Fixed number of digits to have the counter display leading zeros, then click OK.

7 You may wish to type an explanatory note next to the counter.

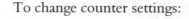

8 Save and publish, and then your visitors will see the new counter when they display your home page.

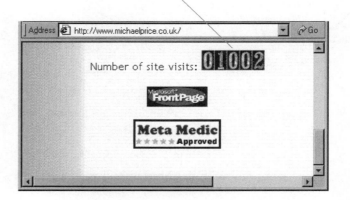

Add a time stamp

You can time stamp one or more pages, but it is more effective to put the stamp in the bottom margin, and a stamp will appear on every page.

Add a time stamp to a page to display the date or the time and date that the page was last published. This tells visitors that the site is up to date and active, and encourages them to pay return visits or to recommend your site to others.

To add the time stamp:

1 Open the web and the home page and select Format, Shared Borders.

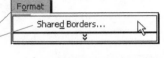

2 Check that the All pages option is specified, and add a bottom border.

3 Click the Comment field to highlight it and press Insert, Date and Time.

You can choose the Date Last Edited, or the Date Last Updated by FrontPage (the date published).

4 Select your preferred format for date and time. Use the text version of the month, to avoid confusion between the USA and UK date formats.

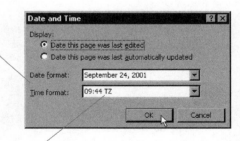

5 If you choose a time, use the TZ (Time Zone) format since the time will be shown in local time at the web server.

The time shown in Normal or Preview views will be the local time for the PC on which you are running FrontPage.

6 Add an expression such as *Last edited on* to qualify the date and time value, and Centre the text in the border.

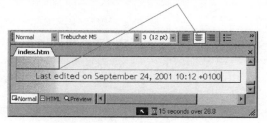

If the website is already open in the browser when you publish an update, press Refresh to rebuild the screen.

7 Save and close the page, and republish the web to the web server. The home page and borders are transferred, and the borders in all the other pages are updated.

The date and time shown in the browser will be the local time for the server. In this case it is a UK server and therefore the same time zone.

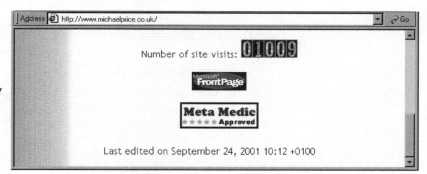

8 Switch to another page in the web, and you'll see the same bottom border but with date applicable to that page:

Make a practice of editing the important pages on the web, or the time stamp will get out of date and spoil the effect of your web.

Horizontal lines

You can add a horizontal line to a page, to separate items or add effect. For example, to add a line above the time stamp:

When you add a horizontal line to a page with a theme specified, the style of the line is dictated by the particular theme being used.

1 Position the cursor before the text and select Insert, Horizontal Line.

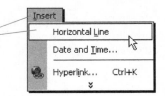

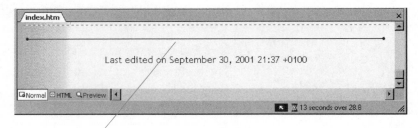

When you add a line to a page that has no theme specified, you get a plain line with no embellishments. However, you can make changes to its properties:

2 Double-click the line, to display the Line Properties panel, set Width as a percent of the window or by pixel count, set the Height in pixels, set the Alignment and choose a colour.

If the current page uses a theme, you can change only the alignment of the line. All other properties are greyed out.

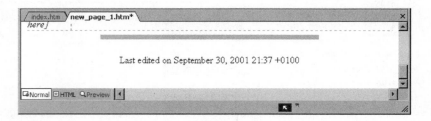

If you select a colour instead of Automatic, you cannot apply shading and the line will always be solid, whatever the background.

Background sound

This is not supported by all web browsers. Remember also that some visitors may be deterred by audio effects.

You can set a background sound which plays when the visitor opens the page.

To specify the sound:

1 Right-click the page, and select Page Properties and then the General tab.

2 In the Background sound Location box, type the path and name for the sound file you want to play (or click Browse to find the file).

You can use Wav files or the compressed MP3 files for short sound extracts, but if you have Midi files for music, they are much better because they are so much smaller.

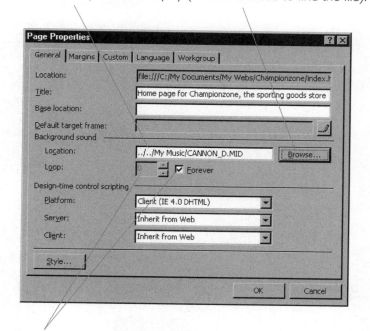

When you save the web page, you'll also be asked to import the sound file. Store this in the web folder, in a Sounds subfolder if you have one set up, so that the file will be available to online visitors.

3 Clear Forever and select 1 or more plays in Loop if you want the sound to play for a limited time.

4 Republish the web, and the sound will play each time that the associated page is selected (assuming that audio effects are enabled within the visitor's browser).

List effects

1 Open the Links page. Organise the links by inserting suitable category headings.

2 Select the links and headings and click to create a single level list.

3 Select a group of links beneath a heading, and click twice, to introduce a second level list.

4 Repeat for each heading in turn, until all the groups are restructured.

Bulleted lists are useful but when there are many items in the lists, you may need a better way to present the information.

...cont'd

Collapsible lists are supported by Microsoft Internet Explorer 4.0 or higher, or other web browsers that support Dynamic HTML.

5 Right-click the top level heading and select List Properties from the context menu displayed, and choose the Picture Bullets tab.

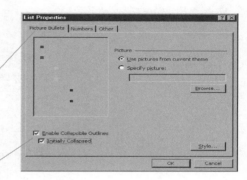

6 Tick Enable Collapsible Outlines, and set them as Initially Collapsed.

7 Save the changes to the page, and click Preview in Browser to see how the page appears to visitors:

The list is shown collapsed initially. Click on any level to expand it to show the next level of detail. Click again to contract it and hide the detail.

Add a note on the page to explain to the visitor about the collapsible lists and how to activate them.

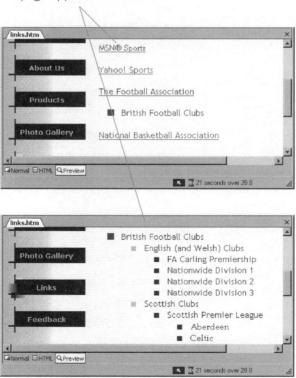

Display form results

1 Open the Feedback page, right-click the form, select Form Properties, and click the Options button.

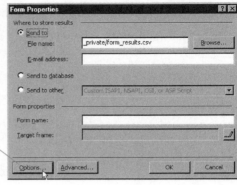

2 Specify the file name for the optional second file, and choose the HTML format. The file will be stored in the root of the web.

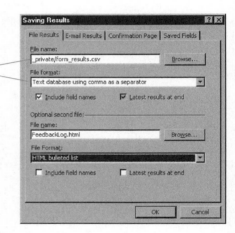

3 Choose which of the fields to show on the results. For example, you may decide not to display T2, the email address. In any event, you won't want to show B1, the button field, which has no associated data value.

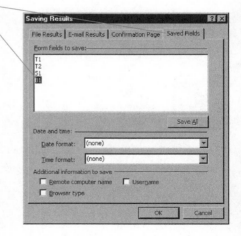

4 Add a hyperlink to the page, targeted at the results file, with an appropriate text message. Save the changes to the web page and republish the web to the server.

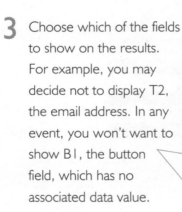

5 Connect to the Internet, open the website, switch to the Feedback page, and click the link to see comments from visitors.

The results are displayed as a HTML page. Note that the late comments entered may not appear immediately — it depends on how the data is cached on the server. Press the Back button to return to the web page.

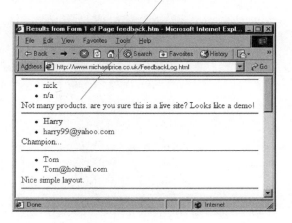

If all you want is to capture visitor comments and make them available to everyone, without any additional data, you can use the predefined Guest Book template.

The Web Site and Web Page templates will provide many of the most needed features, and you can always tailor the pages to add your own particular requirements.

6 Select New, Page or Web, and select the Guest Book web page. This provides a comments area, and saves the data in a log file.

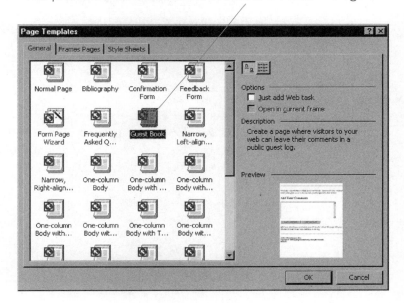

Using colour

A picture may be worth a thousand words, but everyone may not get the same message. There are differences between video adapters and monitors, not just the settings chosen, but in the way they portray colours. Browsers may reinterpret colour schemes, and different types may not follow the same rules. There is also a wide variation in the way individuals perceive colours. When you select colour depth, allocate colours to web components or choose a theme, try to imagine what different types of visitors will see, and make choices that will encourage them to revisit your site.

PCs can display colours selected from over 16 million combinations, using the true colour 32-bit setting. In practice many users will restrict their display to the de facto standard for Windows and the Internet, choosing the 8-bit, 256 colour setting.

The GIF file image format uses 256 colours, so when you save an image to GIF, the graphics program may use dithering. This mixes some of the available colours in a mottled or checkerboard effect, to approximate other colours. Also, if the PC is set for 256 colours, the browser will use a fixed 256 colour palette and may simulate missing colours by dithering.

These changes may degrade the image, especially with large blocks of single colours.

To avoid the effect, you should create or modify the image to use the same 256 colour palette as one of the main browsers. Netscape uses six shade levels of red, green and blue (0, 51, 102, 153, 204 and 255) to give 216 colours, known as the browser-safe palette (see http://www.lynda.com/hex.htm). Internet Explorer honours most of these colours also.

The Browser-Safe Color Palette
By Lynda Weinman

To enhance the effect of your graphics and images, use a transparent colour to make them stand out, especially when your page has a background picture or pattern.

You can choose any suitable colour, it does not have to be white. You should choose a background colour that is not vital to the integrity of the image.

To choose a transparent colour:

1   Open the page, add an image and select it to display the Picture toolbar. Then click the button for selecting the transparency colour.

2   Move the pointer to the colour you want to use, and click to select it. The rest of the image appears superimposed on the page.

You also use transparency colour to create a background, partially transparent image to act as a watermark on the page, and overlay it with text or other images.

3   When your changes are complete, save the page, storing the new image in the Images folder, and republish the web.

Print a page

You can print any FrontPage HTML file from Page view, including the results of forms that have been saved in HTML format.

When you print the current page to the Windows printer, the results depend on which view you start from.

1 In Page view, click the Normal tab and select File, to see the Windows Page Setup, Print Preview and Print options.

When you print from Normal view, you'll get collapsible lists in their fully expanded form.

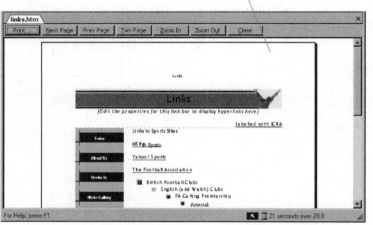

2 Click the HTML tab and File, Print Preview or File, Print will show the actual HTML code that generates the web page.

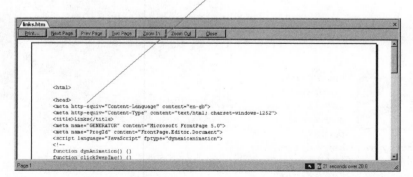

You won't see any of the images that belong to the web page, but you will see the file names and the HTML control statements.

This will print the page as visitors see it, showing for example collapsible lists in the state selected by the visitor. By default, they will be fully collapsed.

3 Click the Preview tab and you'll find the File, Print and Print Preview options disabled (greyed out). You'll need to Preview in Browser to print the page.

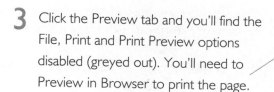

4 The Browser File, Print options available depend on which browser version and level you are using.

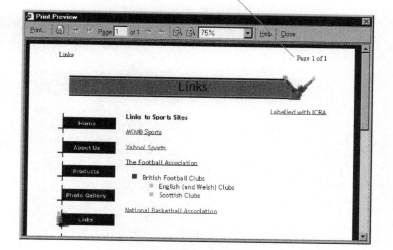

You can print the navigation structure of the current web if you switch to Navigation view and select File, Print.

From the browser, you can select to print specific page frames, if this applies to that particular page (see page 138). You can choose to print all

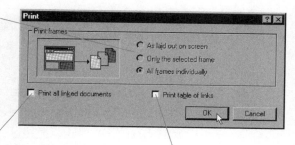

linked documents (take care, there could be a large amount of print) or to print a table of all the URLs on the web page.

Fixing errors

FrontPage uses temporary files on your hard disk to store data about the web. This speeds up the process of opening a large web. However, if you have several authors developing different parts of the web, these files can get out of sync.

To rectify errors that may arise with your web, follow these steps in sequence until the web reports show everything is correct.

I To refresh a page or view, click the Refresh button on the toolbar.

2 Select Tools, and click Recalculate Hyperlinks. For large webs with many hyperlinks, this process may be time-consuming.

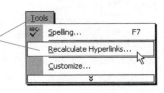

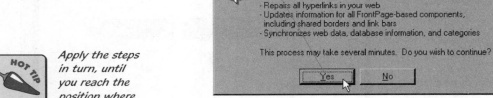

Apply the steps in turn, until you reach the position where your reports show full and correct information about the web.

3 On the Tools menu, click Web Settings, click the Advanced tab, and then click Delete Files.

The next time you open the web on the server, it may taker longer, since FrontPage must copy the web information from the server to recreate your local temporary files.

Upgrading webs

If you have an existing web, it can take advantage of FrontPage 2002 design and publishing features, even if it was created in a previous version of FrontPage, or in a totally different HTML editor. If your web server has the FrontPage extensions, you can upgrade the web to exploit them.

Covers

Chapter Nine

Import the web

If you have an existing web you can import it into FrontPage 2002. You can import the original source files and folders from the hard disk, or you can import the web pages and components from the web server on your network or on the Internet and store them in a FrontPage 2002 web.

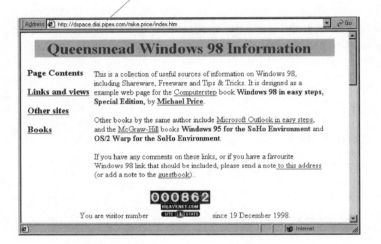

Start FrontPage, close any open webs, and select File, Import.

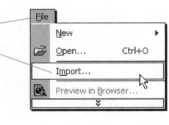

2 Click the Import Web Wizard, specify the name and location for the web you will be creating, and click OK.

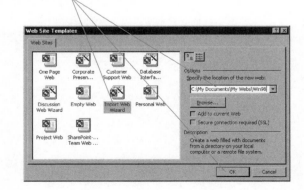

3 When the Import Web Wizard starts, select the location, and enter the path for the web you want to import.

For a source directory, specify the folder on your hard disk or network drive. For a web on the Internet, specify the full URL.

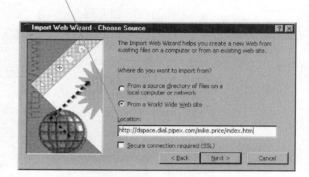

4 Specify the no. of levels below the starting page and a limit on how much disk space to use. Choose to import text and images only, or all files referenced on the pages selected.

The starting page can be any page in the web, not just the home page, and it will follow every link to the depth specified (but avoiding cyclic references). Note that you will only be downloading the pages that belong to this web, and not pages referenced through external links.

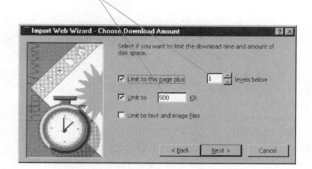

5 Click Finish, and the selected files and folders of the website are copied to the hard disk as a new web.

6 The new web will be shown in FrontPage, ready for you to review or edit as appropriate.

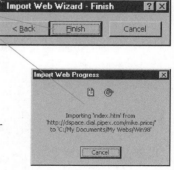

Analyse the web

The downloaded web has been given a FrontPage 2002 folder setup, but all of the files are in the root. It has three image files and three pages. There is no navigation structure defined – only the home page shows.

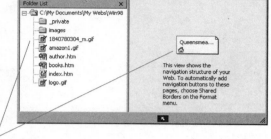

This is typical of the simpler web designs. It uses tables to organise and position text, graphics and links.

One table contains a simulated Navigation bar, linking to pages and bookmarks in the web.

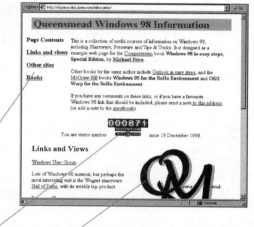

There are links to a hit counter and a guest book.

The graphical image is positioned within a cell of the table, to control its relative placing.

The text tables give the effect of a magazine by simulating columns on the page.

The page is long, so when you scroll down, the navigation table disappears. To make up for this, more scrolling links are provided at the foot of the page. There's also an edit date displayed, and FrontPage will be able to maintain this date.

Web designs take several forms, and you have the opportunity to revise the design when you import a web.

Table structure

This is the simplest and most universal design. Tables provide an easy way to get columns, and align graphics with text. Your visitors don't even see the table because you can hide its borders. Using tables to organise text/graphics on the page

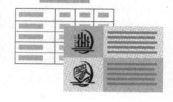

means just about any browsers can display your website. However, it will limit your use of the more advanced web functions.

Shared borders

Shared borders are useful when you want the same items to appear on each page, for example, a company logo or a page banner. They also support navigation bars, as described for the Millennium web, where FrontPage creates and maintains links between the pages. However, they are not very flexible when you want something other than the standard layout.

Frames

Frames allow you to display multiple pages dynamically on one page. They let you display some data continually, such as a list of hyperlinks, and to display a large amount of data that can be scrolled without interfering with other components on the page.

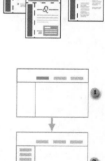

Positioning

Relative and absolute positioning allow you to place text/graphics elements anywhere on a page, independent of paragraph marks, specify layers so that you can overlap text and graphics, and group elements to treat them as a unit. It is the most flexible, can match any requirement but is the hardest to maintain.

Upgrade the web

You do not need to make significant changes to the imported web, in order to upgrade it to FrontPage 2002. In fact, just saving the pages is sufficient. It will support the original design, whether table or frame, and you can use the FrontPage 2002 facilities to manage the web, make editorial changes to the contents as needed, and publish the upgraded web back to the web server. For example, you could check the accuracy of web hyperlinks, or you could make the web organisation more standard.

1 With the imported web open, select Reports from the Views bar, and check the status of the web. For example, verify all hyperlinks.

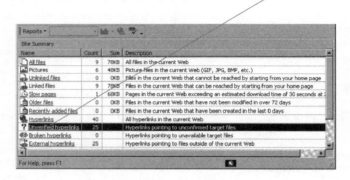

2 With the imported web open, select Folders from the Views bar, and click the root folder of the web.

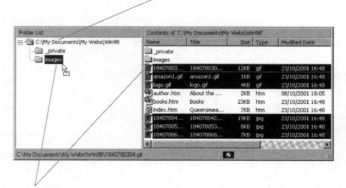

3 Press Ctrl and select all the image files. Drag them, and drop them into the Image folder.

Some changes will be required, if you want to convert to shared borders.

4 Right-click a file name, select Properties and check the page title. A shorter title is better for navigation bars.

If the web you have downloaded includes manual navigation data, you can change to the FrontPage Shared Borders and Navigation Bars, to ensure that the links will be automatically managed in future.

5 Select the Navigation view, click the home page, and drag the second level page files to the appropriate position in the navigation structure.

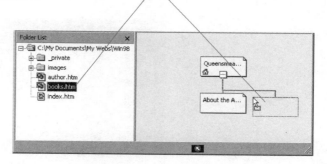

You can use shared borders and navigation bars as described on pages 60–61, to automate the links between pages. Remember that when you've completed the upgrade, you should remove the manual navigation table data that is included in the text of the pages.

Avoid the use of navigation bars if you are planning to use frames (see page 138), since the combination creates confusion in navigating the web.

6 Select Format, Shared Borders and choose which borders and navigation buttons you want, then adjust the Navigation bar properties.

Frames page

The frames page itself contains no visible content. It is merely a container that specifies which other pages to display and how to display them. You click a hyperlink on a page in one frame, and the linked page is displayed in another frame, the *target* frame.

1 First rename the *Index.htm* file to *Main.htm* – the frame page will be the new *Index.htm*.

2 Select Page view and click File, New, Page, Page Template.

3 Click the Frames Pages tab, and preview the templates. It gives a description and preview when you click on any of the templates.

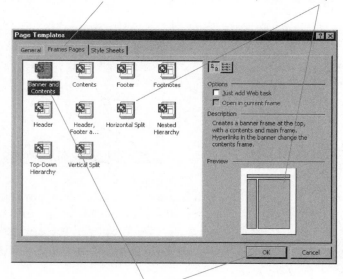

4 Select the Banner and Contents template and click OK. This will create a frames page with three frames, ready for you to set the initial page, or define a new page in each frame.

Select or create the pages to display initially in each of the frames.

5 Save the frames page as *Index.htm*, and select New Page for the top banner frame.

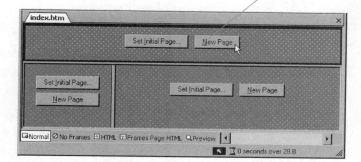

6 Enter the banner title for the website, format the text as Heading 1 and Centre, and save the page as *Banner.htm*.

7 Click New Page on the left, save it as *Contents.htm*, and click Insert, Web Components, Table of Contents.

You must specify the starting page for the TOC, and select the rules that will apply e.g. don't show unlinked pages, and recalculate the table when other pages are edited.

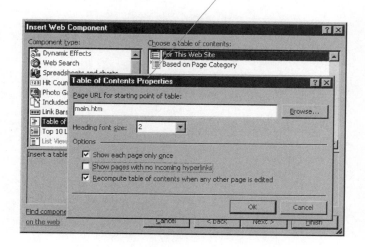

The main page

1 Click Set Initial Page in the right hand frame, and specify the page file *Main.htm* (the original *Index.htm*).

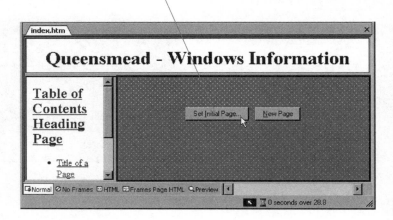

2 Edit the page, Remove the components no longer required, split the text to create new pages, taking advantage of frames facilities.

3 Remove the banner text heading.

4 Remove the contents table.

5 Create pages for Links and Websites.

6 Select each table, and click Table, Convert, Table to Text to remove the table and leave the text freestanding.

This does not add the pages to the Table of Contents. Pages must be linked, directly or indirectly, from the starting page.

7 Add the new pages in Navigation view, to show where they fit in the web structure.

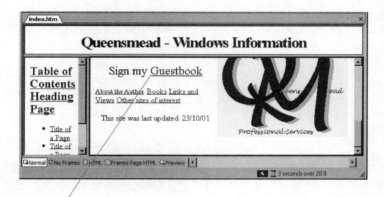

You might wish to copy these links onto all the pages, to help visitors with older browsers (see page 75).

8 Add links to all the pages at the foot of the Main page. Save the changes, and press Preview in Browser to see the revised layout.

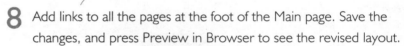

Linked pages are listed in the Table of Contents as well as at the foot of the page.

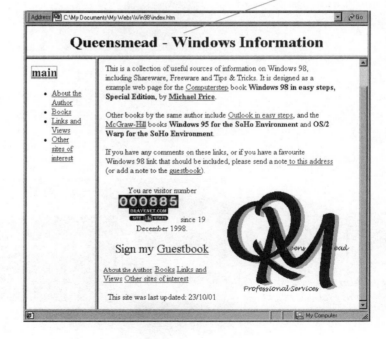

Inline frames

Inline frames are similar to frames pages except that the inline frame and its contents are embedded on an existing web page. Anything that you can put on a regular page you can put in an inline frame. Inline frames can also be customised in the same ways as regular frames.

The advantages of using inline frames is that you don't need to create a separate frames page in order to have embedded content.

FrontPage 2002 supports inline frames, which allow you to embed another web page and its contents in an existing page. One advantage of inline frames is that you can have embedded content without having to create separate frames pages.

To embed another web page and its contents in an existing page using inline frames:

1 In Page view, click in the web page where you want to insert the inline frame.

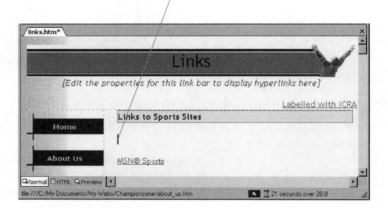

2 Select Insert, Inline Frame and click the Set Initial Page button to open the Insert Hyperlink panel.

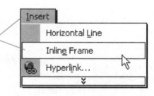

To embed a new page, click the New Page button. A new page will open and you can enter the text and graphics for the page.

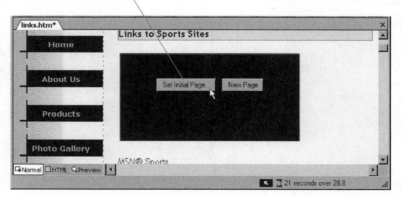

3 From Insert Hyperlink, press Browse to locate the required web page on your site or on the Internet. Click OK.

You can insert a page from your website, or you can insert any URL from the Internet, to give your website a dynamic effect. Here for example, we provide a live link to the BBC Sports football page.

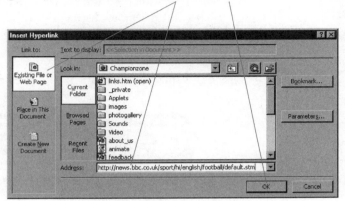

4 Save the page. If you specified a new page, you'll be prompted for a name for the new page file.

You can makes changes to the Name, Initial page, Frame size, Margins, Alignment, Scrollbars and Show border. You can also specify alternate text to show if the visitor's browser does not support frames (see page 144).

5 To make changes to the inline frame, move the cursor over the top border of the inline frame until it changes to a left-pointing arrow, then click to select it, then right-click and choose Inline Frame Properties.

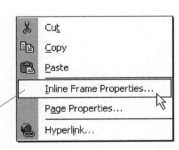

No frames

Older browsers such as Internet Explorer 2 and Netscape 2 do not support Frames pages. The lack of support in web TV is perhaps a more serious restriction. This means that your site may get visitors who are unable to display even the initial home page. FrontPage handles this situation by displaying a simple message to warn the visitor of the problem.

To display the default No Frames message:

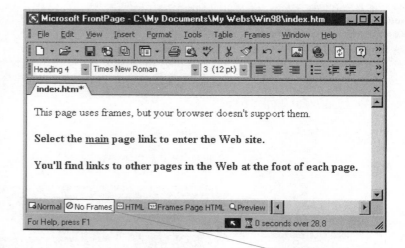

1 Open the Index.htm frames page and click the No Frames tab at the bottom of the display.

2 The first line shows the default message, which provides no alternatives for the visitor.

3 You can add a text message with a hyperlink to a no-frames page. This could be the same Main.htm used for the normal Frames display, or you could create a special no-frames page.

4 If you have added links to the pages (see page 141), you can tell the visitor to use these links to view the contents of your website.

Web designs

You may want several webs at the same ISP, for personal and business use, or for different members of the family, or to suit different browsers. Subwebs make it easy to manage such varying needs.

Covers

Chapter Ten

Web page size

Your website could have just one page or many pages. It depends on how much information you have, and how much you put in each document.

There's no maximum size as such for a page, but you can only display a screenful at a time. If you have a lot of reference material, you should help the visitor to find the main items on the page.

Bookmarks can be used to highlight items of interest, point to sections that are off-screen, and return you to the top of the page.

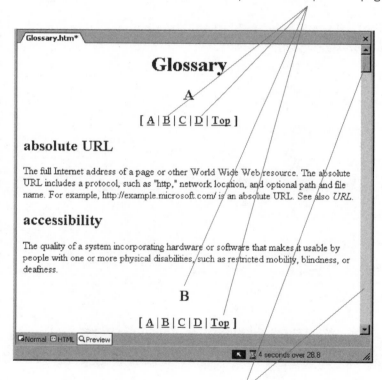

Glossary.htm*

Glossary

A

[A | B | C | D | Top]

absolute URL

The full Internet address of a page or other World Wide Web resource. The absolute URL includes a protocol, such as "http," network location, and optional path and file name. For example, http://example.microsoft.com/ is an absolute URL. See also *URL*.

accessibility

The quality of a system incorporating hardware or software that makes it usable by people with one or more physical disabilities, such as restricted mobility, blindness, or deafness.

B

[A | B | C | D | Top]

Normal HTML Preview

4 seconds over 28.8

2 Scroll bars allow the visitors to select a different portion of the page, or to swiftly scan the page contents.

However, long documents take more time to download, and visitors may fail to spot items that would interest them.

...cont'd

The default screen size is normally assumed to be 800 x 600 pixels. You can split the page up into a number of smaller pages, each providing a screen of information, with little or no scrolling.

An overall index page may be used to set the pages into their proper context.

3 Each page may carry links to all the other pages, or it may just needs links to the next and the previous pages.

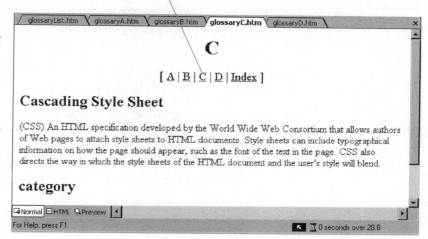

You can arrange the links in navigation bars or tables of contents, if you use shared borders (see pages 60–61) or frames (see pages 138–139).

Choose the page size and style based on the type of information and the type of visitor you expect. There is no single right answer, but there are some guidelines you can consider:

- For overviews and presentations, don't make the page longer than the default window size.

- Use scrollable screens for longer pages, with text or reference lists.

Some users need screen reader software which may need to rearrange the screen content to present it in a logical sequence.

- For general purpose pages, keep the size around one or two screens, and don't hide important features like Continue buttons below the edge of the initial display.

- Consider preparing a separate, single page version of your website for printing/downloading or non-graphical browsers.

- If your website uses frames, consider a separate entry point for users without frame support (or with an aversion to frames).

Web structures

Web space providers and ISPs cater for the standard web structure which is really designed for the single owner situation.

The typical single user personal website has one home page and a number of lower level subsidiary or child pages.

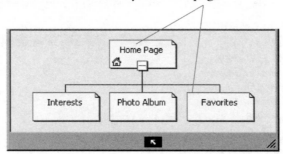

If you are sharing the web space with others, you might require separate home pages for each user, yet manage the site as a unit.

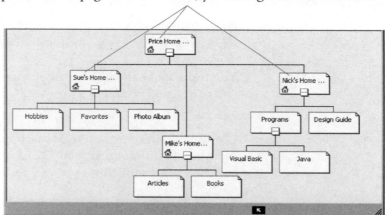

This is in effect what FrontPage offers you, through the subweb facility. You create a master or parent web, and build your independent subwebs within it. Each subweb can have its own settings and themes, and be separately edited. However, the set of subwebs can be published and maintained as a group, to a single ISP or WPP account.

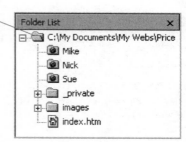

Create the parent

Create a web to act as the entry to the subwebs that you want to create.

I Start FrontPage, close any open webs and select File, New, Page or Web, Web Site Templates.

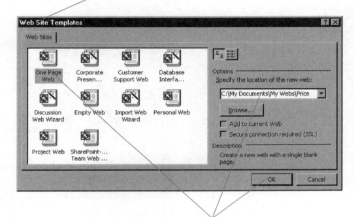

Any type of web, including an existing web, can be used as the parent web for a subweb.

2 Select the One Page Web template, specify the location and the name for the web, and click OK.

The web will be generated with a single blank web page named Index.htm, plus the usual FrontPage folder structure.

3 Open Index.htm in Page view. Add a page title and some text placeholders for the hyperlinks to the subwebs you plan.

It is not essential to put hyperlinks in the parent web, since you can address the subweb directly from the browser. However, for default entry through the parent home page, you do need to add suitable links to the parent.

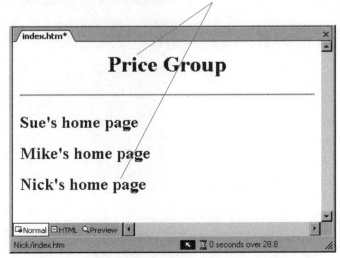

Create subwebs

If the contents for the subweb already exist in another web, then choose the single page web template, and publish the existing web to this new subweb.

Open the parent web. Select File, New, Web, choose the template (e.g. Personal Web), and specify the location as the parent web folder. Add the subweb name.

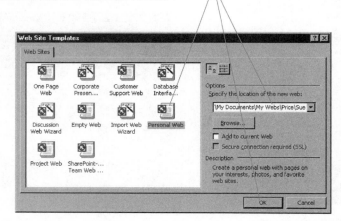

The subweb is created within the parent web, and starter versions of the *Index.htm* page and any other pages will be created.

If you update the web this way, the web settings from the original web will be retained, so you'll have to reapply shared borders and themes.

2 Create the web pages or, if there is an existing web you can publish the contents to the new subweb.

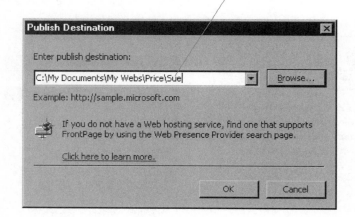

3 Repeat the process for each of the remaining subwebs in turn, to install them below the parent web folder.

Complete the parent web

The subwebs appear as web folders within the parent web folder. You can open the subweb by double-clicking the folder. A new instance of FrontPage will be launched for the subweb; you can edit the files or review the reports, as with any web.

To provide links from the parent to the subwebs (see page 149):

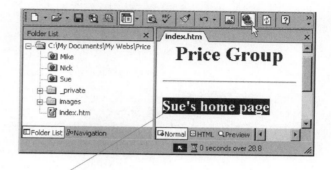

1 Open the parent web, edit the home page *Index.htm*, and highlight a subweb hyperlink placeholder. Click Insert Hyperlink.

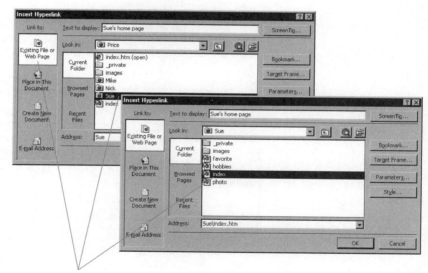

You can set the full URL for the home page, or just the subweb name. See page 152 for the effect on browser previews.

2 Click Existing File or Web Page, and select the appropriate subweb. Click OK to take the subweb name. Alternatively, double-click the subweb to open it, click the home page Index.htm, then click OK.

3 Repeat these steps for each of the hyperlink placeholders in turn.

Preview the webs

1 Open the parent web, open the home page and press Preview in Browser.

2 The home page for the parent web is displayed. Click one of the subweb hyperlinks. The illustration shows both forms of hyperlink.

If you specify just the subweb URL, Preview in Browser will open the folder rather than the web.

When you are online, specifying the web URL with or without the home page will open the web just the same.

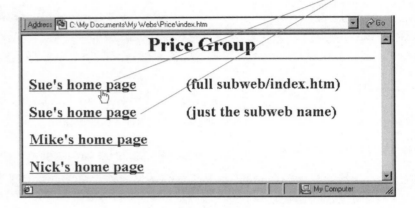

3 The home page displays if the full URL is defined in the hyperlink.

You can still access the web. Double-click the icon for the home page to open the subweb in the normal Internet Explorer manner.

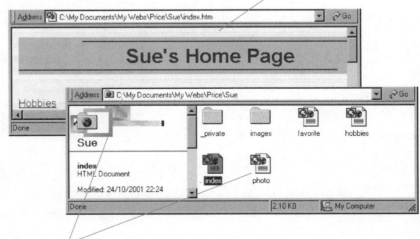

4 The web folder is displayed Windows Explorer style, if the hyperlink contains the web URL without the page name.

Publish the webs

The only real difference when you publish a web with subwebs, is the tick in the box.

I Open the parent web, select File, Publish Web, and sign-on as needed.

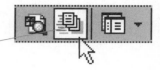

2 Enter the URL for your web server, choose to Publish all pages, and tick Include subwebs. Press the Publish button.

You may find that your ISP or web space provider does not permit you to create subwebs from the FrontPage client:

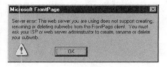

You may however be able to publish each subweb individually, specifying the subweb name as part of the URL.

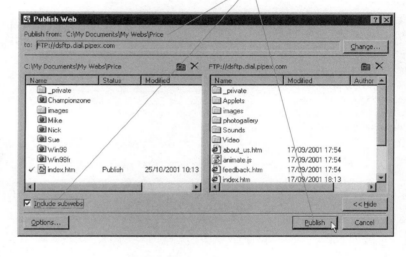

3 The files and folders in the parent web and in the subwebs are copied to the web server.

If you are replacing an existing website, replace the structure. If the web is being maintained by several authors, let FrontPage manage and synchronise changes. FrontPage replaces files and folders with matching names, but it won't delete files and folders no longer being referenced.

4 FrontPage detects conflicts between the existing contents at the website and the new web.

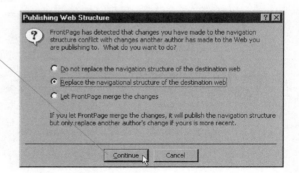

5 When the transfer completes, the new site is ready to use.

Visiting subwebs

1 Select the website in your browser while connected to the Internet, to display the parent home page.

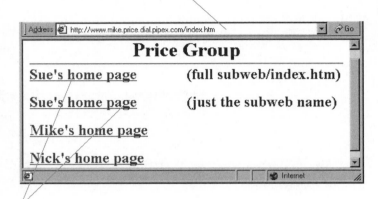

When you provide a URL without a page name, the browser tries the standard names for home pages, and displays the first match it finds, in this case 'Index.htm'.

2 Click on the hyperlink to display one of the subwebs. You'll get the home page even if the link has no page name specified.

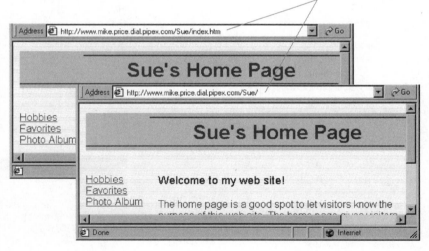

The web folder name usually doesn't matter because it is not published. However, when a web becomes a subweb, the name and its case become an issue. You can remember to tell your contacts what capitalisation to use, but it's better to rename the web folders with lower case names – the normally expected format.

3 However, you must specify the proper case.

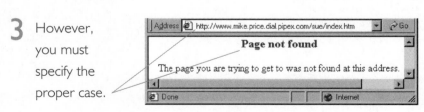

If the web server supports FrontPage Server Extensions, you can view the web folders and make immediate changes to the contents.

To modify a web page:

4 Use your browser to view the page to be changed, and select File, Edit with Microsoft FrontPage.

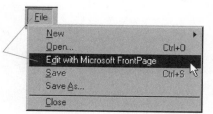

5 You will be asked for your Login name and password to confirm your authority to make changes to the contents of the website.

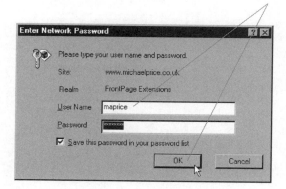

The web page will be opened in FrontPage, ready for editing.

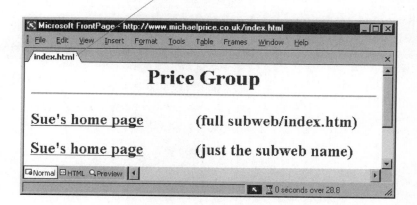

Edit the web remotely

Type the folder and file names exactly as they appear in the web folder, using the correct case.

You can edit the files at the web server without actually opening the website.

1 Select File, Open, specify the website URL and choose Open as Web Folder.

2 When you complete your sign-on, the web folder is displayed, allowing you to locate the subweb and web page to be modified.

You can open folders and subwebs within the web folder to find the pages or image files that you wish to revise.

Working with the web server is very useful when you have two or more people in your group who are allowed to apply changes.

3 Right-click a page file and select Edit to open it in FrontPage and make changes, then choose Save, Close to update the web server.

...cont'd

If you did have the website open in the browser, press the Reload or Refresh button to display the updated version of the page.

4 Double-click the page file icon to open it in the browser and see the changes that you have made.

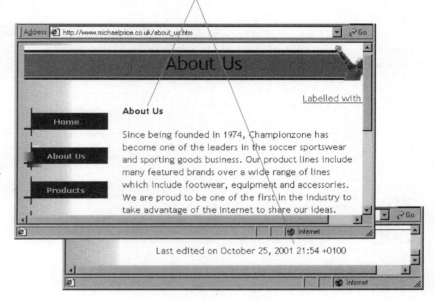

The web page shows the new content and date of modification.

The original copy on your hard disk will not be updated. You'll have to publish the web from the web server to your hard disk to refresh your copy.

If you build a website on a web server that does not support server extensions, you will not be able to view the web folders or edit the files at the web server.

Changes must be made locally on disk and published by FTP to the web server.

5 Select File, Open, specify a web file name and Open as Web Folder. You'll see a message saying that Web Folder view is not allowed, and offering to open in the default view instead.

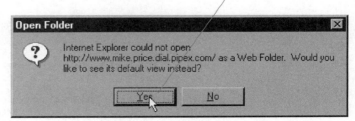

Switching sites

When you change web space providers and move your website to a new web server, you can redirect your visitors to the new location.

1 Replace the existing home page for the old location, with an explanatory message, and a hyperlink to the new location.

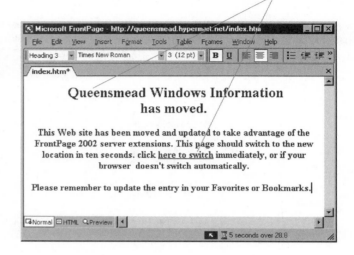

You can use the same technique to redirect visitors to pages within your site, when you reorganise and rename pages, since visitors might bookmark any page on your site, not just the home page.

2 Right-click the page, select Page Properties, Custom, and Add a system meta-variable to refresh the page after ten seconds.

See pages 108–109 for more details on meta-variables.

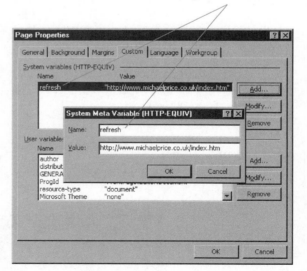

When visitors select your old website or web page, they will see the message and get an automatic transfer to the replacement.

Tables, images and forms

A more detailed look at features of FrontPage, including the use of tables, the design of image maps and the creation of discussion group webs using interactive forms.

Covers

Chapter Eleven

Creating tables

Tables are used in web pages for two different purposes. They are used as a method for arranging text and graphics, as discussed on page 135, and they have their more usual function of presenting text and numeric data.

FrontPage provides several ways of creating tables. You can create a simple table by specifying the number of rows and columns. To create the table, in Page view select the insertion point and:

1 Click the Insert Table button to display the table selector. Click to expand the toolbar if the table button doesn't show.

2 Move the cursor down and across until you've selected the required number of rows and columns. The selector expands if more cells are needed.

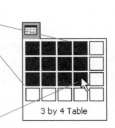

3 Click the bottom right cell to generate the table with default property values set.

4 Right-click the table and choose Table Properties to adjust table settings such as Alignment, Padding, Spacing or Color.

You can modify the properties of the table after creating it. See opposite for examples of layout properties.

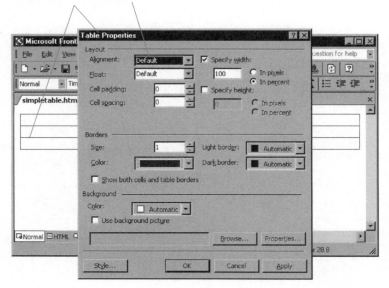

Table properties

If you click the Table button, you get default properties. But you can specify properties for your table as you are creating it, and make these the new defaults if required.

1 From the menu bar select Table then select Insert and Table.

2 Select the number of rows and columns you want, and specify the width of the cells.

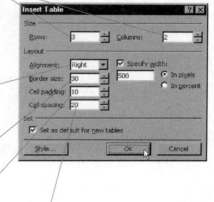

3 Set the Alignment on the page for the table.

4 Enter the width in pixels, to be used for the border.

5 Enter the cell padding (the space within the cell).

6 Enter the cell spacing (the gap between cells).

Layout properties that you specify for the table will be used as the default properties the next time you create a table.

7 Note that you can specify the width of the table in pixels or as a percentage of the screen or frame width.

Draw a table

If you want a complex table, with different sizes of cells and varying numbers of columns and rows, you can draw it the way you want, no matter how irregular.

1 In Page view, select Table, Draw Table, and FrontPage will open the Tables toolbar.

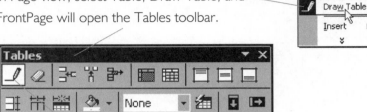

2 Select the Draw Table tool, and draw the outside border of the table by dragging from the upper-left corner to the lower-right.

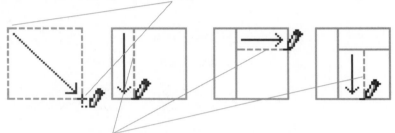

3 Draw vertical and horizontal lines, to create columns and rows in the table, and nested within cells.

Click Draw Table on the Tables toolbar, to deselect the button and end table drawing.

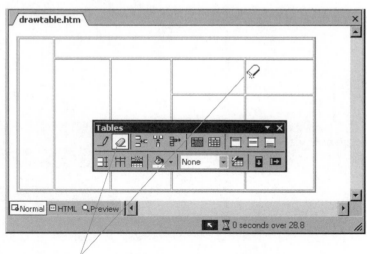

4 Click Eraser on the toolbar, and drag across an unwanted line. When the line turns red, release the mouse button.

Convert text to table

You can convert text into a table if it has been delimited — separated into rows and columns. Use a separator character to mark column boundaries, and the end of line (paragraph marker) to indicate rows.

HTML does not directly support tab characters, so avoid using tab characters as your text delineator.

If you select None, all the text will be placed in a single cell table, for example to keep all selected text together when you use tables for page layout.

The current default values will be used for borders and spacing, but you can change properties, and resize the cells and the columns.

1 Open the web and open the page in Page view. Type or copy the text onto the page.

officexp.htm*

Office XP Suites
Component / Edition, Pro SE, Pro, Std, Dev
Word 2002, Y, Y, Y, Y
Excel 2002, Y, Y, Y, Y
Outlook 2002, Y, Y, Y, Y
PowerPoint 2002, Y, Y, Y, Y
Access 2002 , Y, Y, n, Y
FrontPage 2002, Y, n, n, Y
SharePoint Team Services, Y, n, n, Y
Publisher 2002, Y, n, n, n
IntelliMouse Explorer, Y, n, n, n
Developer Tools, n, n, n, Y

Normal HTML Preview
For Help, press F1   0 second

2 Highlight the text (excluding the title) and select Table, Convert, Text to Table.

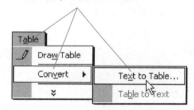

Table

Draw Table
Convert ▶ → Text to Table...
                Table to Text

3 Specify the separator character that you have used and click OK. The table will be created with the no. of columns defined by the row with the most separator characters. Cell sizes will be adjusted to best fit the text:

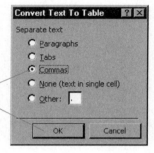

Convert Text To Table

Separate text
○ Paragraphs
○ Tabs
◉ Commas
○ None (text in single cell)
○ Other: [ ]

OK   Cancel

officexp.htm*

Office XP Suites

Component / Edition	Pro SE	Pro	Std	Dev
Word 2002	Y	Y	Y	Y
Excel 2002	Y	Y	Y	Y
Outlook 2002	Y	Y	Y	Y
PowerPoint 2002	Y	Y	Y	Y
Access 2002	Y	Y	n	Y
FrontPage 2002	Y	n	n	Y
SharePoint Team Services	Y	n	n	Y
Publisher 2002	Y	n	n	n
IntelliMouse Explorer	Y	n	n	n
Developer Tools	n	n	n	Y

Normal HTML Preview
For Help, press F1   2 seconds over 28.8

Tables within tables

You can carry out the following additional operations. You can:

- *adjust the entries in an existing table*
- *split a single cell into several rows or columns*
- *remove lines to combine cells*
- *insert a whole table within a cell*

If you select Table, Insert Rows or Columns, you can choose to insert above or below the selected cell, and you can specify how many rows you want.

1 Click in the first row and click the Insert Row button on the Table toolbar to add a row above the selected row.

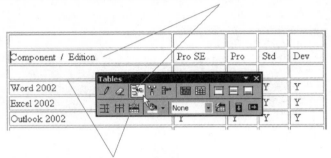

2 Click in the next row, and click the Insert Row button, to put another row into the table.

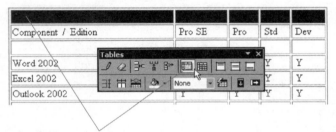

3 Highlight the whole of the first new row and click the Merge Cells button, to combine them all into one wide cell.

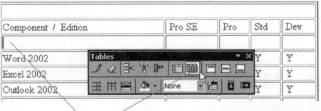

4 Select the first cell in the second new row, click the Split cells button, and choose Split into columns, setting the number as 2.

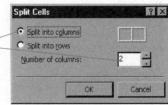

5 Select all the cells except the first cell in the second new row, which is now row three in the table.

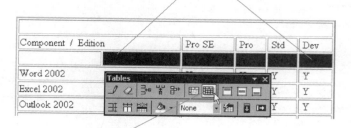

You can also select Tables from the menu bar and choose Split cells to display this panel to define how you want to split the selected cell or cells.

6 Click the Split cells button and this time choose Split into rows. Again set the number to 2.

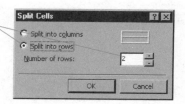

7 Enter the title, centre it, and enter the subtitles and data values.

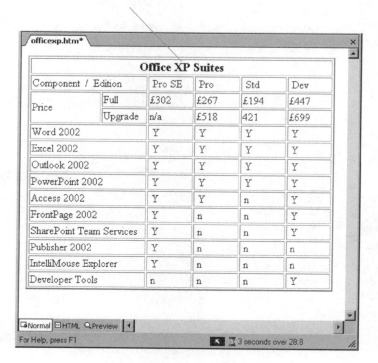

Office XP Suites					
Component / Edition		Pro SE	Pro	Std	Dev
Price	Full	£302	£267	£194	£447
	Upgrade	n/a	£518	421	£699
Word 2002		Y	Y	Y	Y
Excel 2002		Y	Y	Y	Y
Outlook 2002		Y	Y	Y	Y
PowerPoint 2002		Y	Y	Y	Y
Access 2002		Y	Y	n	Y
FrontPage 2002		Y	n	n	Y
SharePoint Team Services		Y	n	n	Y
Publisher 2002		Y	n	n	n
IntelliMouse Explorer		Y	n	n	n
Developer Tools		n	n	n	Y

Image map and hotspots

You can associate a hyperlink with a section of a graphic, so that when you click that part of the image, it switches you to the specified URL. If the image has several distinct areas, you may want a different hyperlink for each. Each activated area is known as a hotspot, and an image with one or more hotspots defined is known as an image map.

Before defining hotspots, you may want to specify a default hyperlink for the parts of the image not otherwise defined.

1 Select Insert, Picture, From File, to add the image onto the page. Click the image to select it, showing the picture handles.

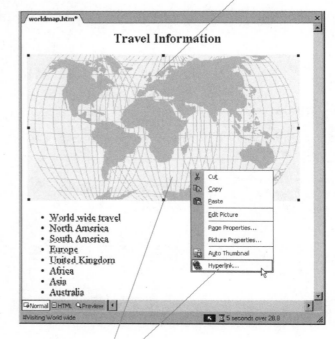

See page 32 for more details about defining hyperlinks and creating bookmarks on the page.

2 Right-click the image and select Hyperlink from the menu. Define the URL for a web page or for a bookmark to a location on the current page.

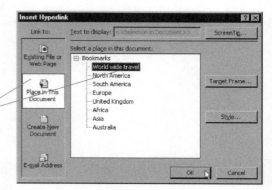

This link will be the default for the image, and will be associated with any area of the picture not separately defined as a hotspot.

You can define a rectangle, circle or polygon shape. For a close fit, choose the polygon and take a series of small steps.

3 Click the picture. If the Picture toolbar does not appear, click View, Toolbars to display it. On the toolbar, click one of the Hotspot shapes.

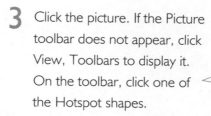

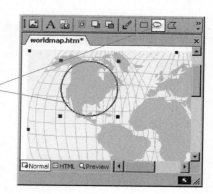

4 Draw the shape onto the image. When you release the mouse button, the Insert Hyperlink panel appears.

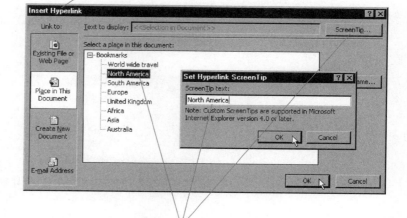

Any parts of the image not covered by a hotspot will take on the default hyperlink address.

5 Enter the URL or select a bookmark for the hotspot. Click Screen Tip to add a text prompt for visitors.

Repeat the drawing and hyperlink definition for each hotspot region, until the map is complete.

6 As you'll find in Preview, the hotspot is hidden, but a hyperlink flag shows when you move the mouse over it, and the screen tip is shown.

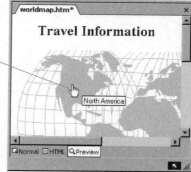

Text hotspots

A text hotspot is a string of text that you place on the image and assign a hyperlink.

If the image type is in a different format, a GIF format version will be created.

In this example, the image hotspots link to bookmarks in a collapsible list.

1 Click the picture, and select the Text button from the Picture toolbar.

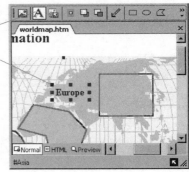

2 Click the image, and type the desired entry in the text box.

3 Double-click the edge of the text box to display the Insert Hyperlink screen, and add the link and screen tip.

4 Only the text hotspots (and the screen tip) will be visible in Preview or when the page is viewed in the browser.

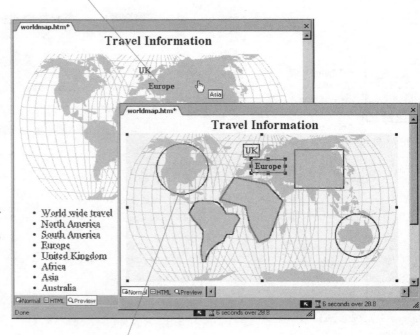

5 Select Normal view and click the image to see the hotspot areas.

Set up a discussion group

You can use the Discussion Web wizard to create a web with the features you want.

As well as providing information to your visitors, you can set up an environment for them to communicate with each other, in the form of a discussion group or forum that provides:

- A table of contents with hyperlinks to articles and responses.

- A search form to find particular words or phrases.

- An entry form for a visitor to type an article or response.

- Threaded replies, to connect related articles and responses.

Adding a discussion group to an existing web

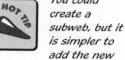

You could create a subweb, but it is simpler to add the new pages as an extension to your current web.

1 Open the web into which you will put the discussion group.

2 Select File, New, Page or Web and click Website Templates in the New from template section.

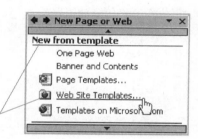

3 Select the Discussion Web Wizard and choose to add the new pages to the current web.

The Wizard helps you define all the pages needed, for articles, searches and responses, plus a table of contents. Some of the steps in the process are shown on page 170.

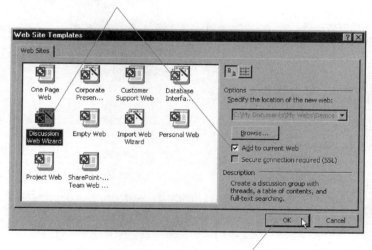

4 The wizard guides you through the process to creating the group.

Discussion group wizard

The Wizard asks questions to help you create a discussion forum as a web of linked pages in which visitors can post articles and replies.

Folders whose names begin with an underscore are hidden. This will help keep the discussion documents separate from other web content.

If you are adding pages to an existing web, don't set the discussion Contents as the home page, or it will overwrite the existing one. However, you must add a link to the Contents page on your current home page, so visitors can join in.

Click Finish at any point and the discussion group will be set up with the default answers.

In the final dialog, choose No Frames or Dual interface so that visitors can even take part in the discussion if their browser doesn't support frames.

1 You must have a submissions form but the TOC, Search Form, Threaded Replies and Confirmation Page are optional.

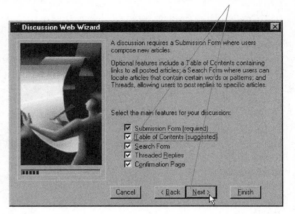

2 Enter a descriptive title for the forum, and specify the name of the folder in your web where all the responses will be stored.

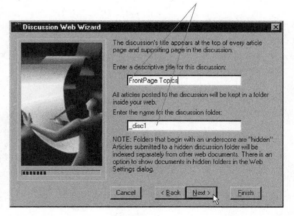

3 You'll automatically get Subject and Comments as input fields for the submission form. You can optionally select Category or Products, and you can add more fields later if required.

4 In the next dialog, pick a TOC sort (preferably Newest to oldest). The search form will report the found articles by listing the subject and optionally size, date and score (closeness to the search criteria).

Discussion group web

Depending on the choices you made while running the Wizard, you will see frames or pages for the forms. In addition to Contents and Post, you may find Confirmation and Search forms.

As well as posting messages or articles, visitors can reply to previous articles in the discussion, creating conversation threads.

You can edit and delete articles posted to the discussion group by selecting the option to show documents in hidden directories, in Advanced Web settings.

You must publish the web to a web server with the FrontPage Server Extensions before you can operate with the forms.

Like other FrontPage forms, the discussion group requires the Server Extensions to be installed on the web server.

When the wizard ends, it identifies the main pages in the new discussion groups as the FrontPage Topics Table of Contents (TOC) and the Post (submission) form:

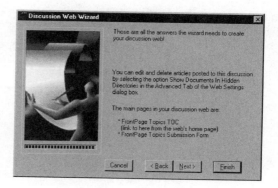

1 Open the web, open the Index page and select Folder List to view the files that have been added to the web.

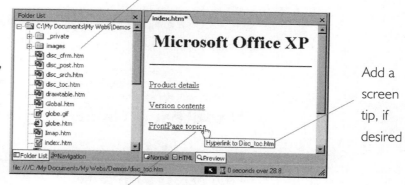

Add a screen tip, if desired

2 Create a text entry on the Index page and associate it with a hyperlink to the discussion group table of contents *Disc_toc.htm*.

3 Switch to Preview and click on the link to open the Contents page. Note the discussion group subject heading and navigation links.

4 Finally, the Post page allows a visitor to create a message or article that will be stored at your website, entering the subject, the visitor's name, and the comment text, then pressing the Post button.

Web conversations

1 At the web server, your visitors will see the list of messages, with their dates, authors, subjects and conversation threads.

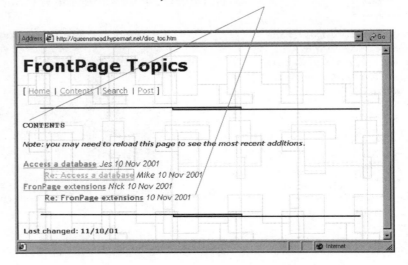

2 Click on a message to display it, and reply direct to it, or post a new item, or view Next or Previous.

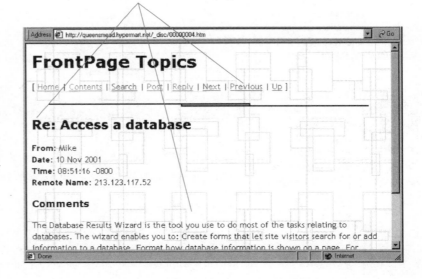

3 Select the Search page to look for specific topics using keywords.

Sources of help

There is a wealth of information about web design on the Internet: from Microsoft, from other hardware and software suppliers and from interested groups such as universities. You'll find free, demo or trial add-ins for FrontPage that make the design task easier.

Covers

Chapter Twelve

Local help

The first place to look for advice and information on using FrontPage is provided as part of the product.

1 Select Help, Microsoft FrontPage Help (or click the Help button on the toolbar, or type a query in the Ask a Question box).

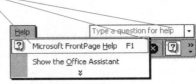

2 Click [+] to expand sections, and [-] to collapse them.

There are sections in Help to cover all the aspects of designing, enhancing and publishing a website.

Note that some of the pages are actually stored on the Internet. You must have an active connection to view these.

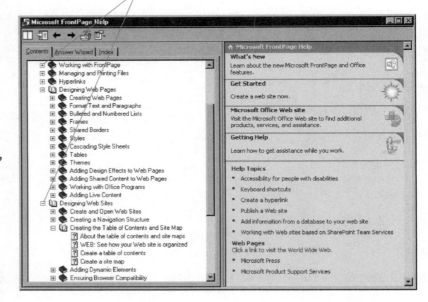

3 You can Hide the Contents list panel, to allow more room for the selected topic.

You can copy an item such as a table or a form field from the Help example to paste it into one of your own pages in Page view.

4 View the Glossary at the end of the contents list, for definitions and explanations of terms.

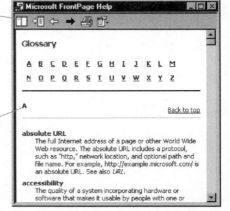

Office on the Web

In addition to the web page references, there is also a link to help on the Internet, via the Office Update facility.

1 Select Help, Office on the Web. This starts your Internet connection, if required, and displays the Office XP Assistance Centre home page.

2 From this page you can:

- Follow the links for top tips, articles and additional assistance.
- Get help with any highlighted Office XP activities.
- Obtain Office XP updates and downloads.
- Access the Design gallery and get Office templates and eServices.

The contents of these pages will change on a regular basis, so the pages that you see when you select Office on the Web will be different.

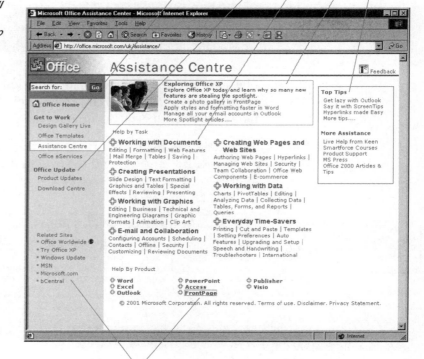

This site will be the source for fixes and enhancements to FrontPage 2002 and the other Office XP applications.

3 You can also visit related websites or choose a product-specific web page, including the link to FrontPage assistance.

FrontPage assistance

If you've set up your system for UK operation, the Office on the Web menu entry will display the UK version of the Assistance Centre. The links however will be USA versions, such as the FrontPage Assistance Center.

Select FrontPage from the Help By Product list, to see a list of articles that cover or reference FrontPage topics.

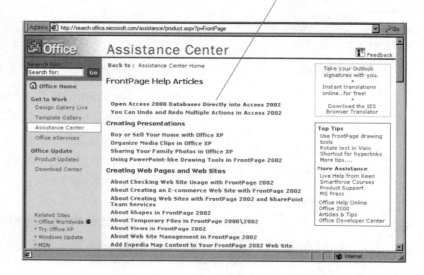

The areas covered include creating presentations, creating web pages and websites, email and collaboration, everyday timesavers, and working with data, documents and graphics.

As an example, there's an article on creating an e-commerce website with FrontPage and the bCentral Commerce Manager Add-in:

The bCentral Commerce Manager Add-in for FrontPage allows you to create product department pages, product lists, and product detail pages for your e-commerce website, making it easier for customers visiting your site to purchase your products.

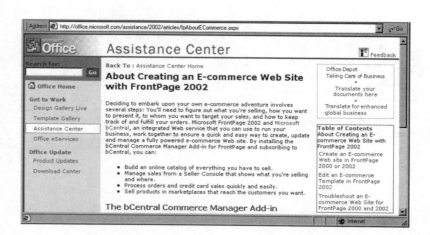

The Download Center

There are downloads for older previous FrontPage versions as well, and some downloads apply to many of the Office programs.

1 Click Download Center, choose the FrontPage product and the 2002/XP version, and select the type(s) of download you want.

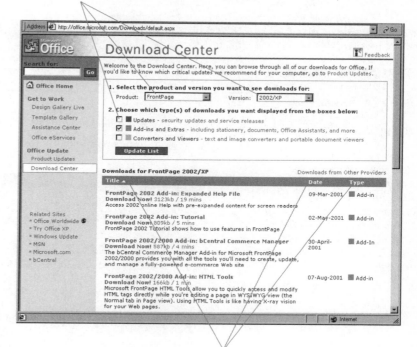

Click Read this first for details of the add-in functions, setup and use.

2 Click the header to sort by title, date or type. The file size and download time are shown. Click Download Now to obtain a copy.

3 Click Downloads from other providers. Click the FrontPage link to list third party add-in programs.

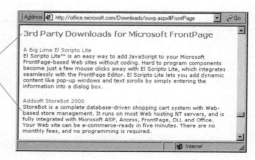

When you select Download Now, the required files are transferred to your hard disk, ready for you to install the add-in or update.

The specific products and options listed will vary from time to time, but you should expect to find trial versions of third party add-in applications, such as the El Scripto Lite.

Download an add-in

The security settings in your browser may be set to High, and prevent you from downloading files from the Download Center:

Make the Download Center a trusted website using a security setting of Medium, or temporarily reduce your browser security to Medium, download the add-in(s) of your choice and then reset browser security to High.

1 To download an add-in from the Download Center, locate the required file and click the Download Now! link.

> **FrontPage 2002/2000 Add-in: HTML Tools**   07-Aug-2001 ■ Add-in
> **Download Now!** 166kb / 1 min
> Microsoft FrontPage HTML Tools allow you to quickly access and modify HTML tags directly while you're editing a page in WYSIWYG view (the Normal tab in Page view). Using HTML Tools is like having X-ray vision for your Web pages.

2 Choose to save the file to your hard disk, and select a suitable folder to hold your FrontPage related downloads.

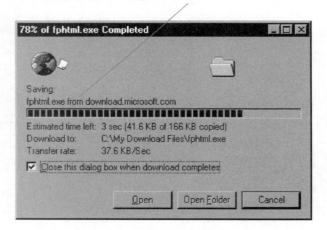

J-Bots Plus 2002 is a collection of components that create navigation menus, mouse overs, scrolling messages, page redirects, floating windows, and banner ads, without you having to program, since J-Bots write and place the JavaScript code on the page. See page 180 for more details.

3 You can download add-ins from the third party providers in a similar fashion, though you may be requested to provide contact details before getting access to the downloads for trial versions.

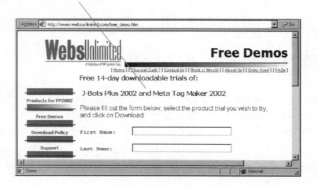

Install an add-in

An add-in extends FrontPage by adding custom commands or specialised functions. You can obtain add-ins from independent software vendors.

1 Find the downloaded module in the folder that you specified for FrontPage related downloads, and double-click to run the install.

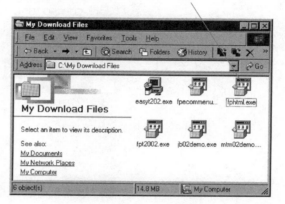

2 Respond to the prompts, and the add-in is installed and activated.

For some add-ins, you may need to close FrontPage before you can install.

3 Select Tools, Add-Ins to start the Add-In Manager and view the list of add-ins that are available.

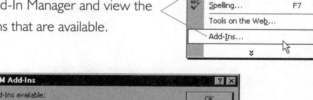

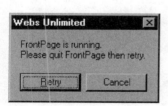

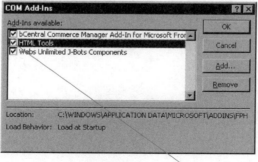

4 Click in the box to disable or to re-enable the particular add-in.

Using J-Bots

The J-Bots add-in is a 14 day trial version with just a small number of components. You can upgrade to a full version of 25 or 50 components.

1 Select Insert, J-Bots Components and select one of the six groups, for example General, then pick one of the items, for example the Global Clock component.

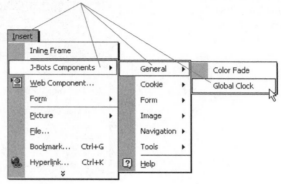

2 Alternatively, you can select the group and the specific component, using the buttons of the J-Bots Components toolbar.

Perhaps not the best item to include as a sample, since the Global Clock doesn't seem to understand British Summer Time.

3 Select the format styles for the time, add separators and text as required, choose the time zone and click Generate to enter the appropriate code onto the page.

Select Preview or Preview in Browser, to see the results with the actual times displayed.

4 You can generate several different entries, if you want to show the time in various places.

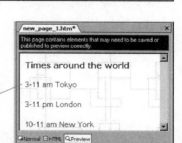

More information from MS

There's a lot more detail on FrontPage offered from the main Microsoft websites.

You will find many web pages devoted to FrontPage at various Microsoft websites. These are mainly USA sites, but there are some local sites also devoted to FrontPage.

1 For product information, visit the USA FrontPage product web page at http://www.microsoft.com/frontpage/default.htm.

There are links to support pages and related products, and also a link to Assistance Center and Office Update (see page 175).

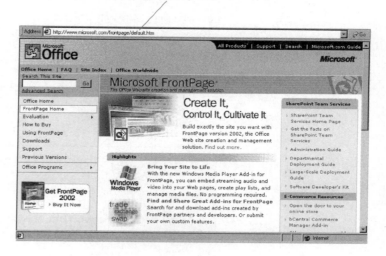

2 For UK based information, visit the Microsoft UK web pages at http://www.microsoft.com/uk/office/frontpage.htm.

From here you can subscribe to various free Office newsletters, including the monthly FrontPage Bulletin (see page 182).

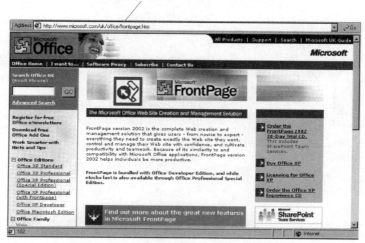

FrontPage Bulletin

When you register for the monthly FrontPage Bulletin from Microsoft you can select a plain text or HTML format. It will be sent as an email message to the email address that you specify.

1 From the Microsoft FrontPage website, choose to register for a free newsletter.

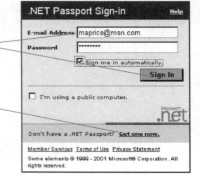

2 You must have a Passport ID in order to register with Microsoft. This is available at no charge.

3 Select the newsletters that you wish to receive. You must have a Passport ID in order to complete the registration.

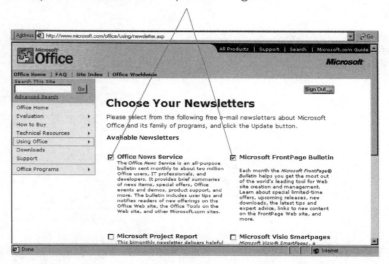

There are similar regular newsletters for other Microsoft products or for special interest groups such as developers.

The bulletin is issued on a monthly basis and covers a variety of information concerning FrontPage and related products. The topics covered include:

- News about additions, updates and fixes.

- Details of special offers, demos and trial software.

- Links to FrontPage information sites and web services.

- Tips, tricks, tutorials and expert advice.

Every month, several websites are picked to showcase the use of FrontPage. Visit them to help you identify practices that you admire (or ones that you would prefer to avoid).

4 Select one of the example websites based on FrontPage that are listed in FrontPage bulletins, e.g. www.pasadenasymphony.org.

You can view back issues of the bulletins, at the Archive website which can be found at:

http://www.microsoftfront page.com/bulletin/archive/ index.html

5 Select File, Edit with Microsoft FrontPage, to view the structure of any page in the website (NB: click Cancel on password request).

You can save parts of the example website to help you build or extend your own web, though you should use hyperlinks rather than full copies to share another site with your visitors.

6 If you wish, you can select File, Save As to save the contents of the web page, HTML code and images to your hard disk.

FrontPage websites

The World Wide Web is a very dynamic environment so don't be surprised if the URLs you see mentioned here have been renamed or removed by the time you visit them.

A search for FrontPage 2002 using www.google.com or similar search engines should give you a wide range of related sites.

1 For a variety of FrontPage 2002 related news, information, tips and tricks, tools and templates, visit http://www.frontpage2002.com/.

2 If you want ideas for website design and Internet marketing, e-commerce and affiliates, visit http://www.frontpageworld.com/.

Click the link What's New for a list of recent additions to the FrontPage World website, or click Tips for a shortcut to the Tips and tricks section.

3 You can sign up for a free newsletter at this site. You'll also find numerous links to other FrontPage 2002 related sites.

Design guides

When you view any design guides on the Internet, be sure to check the date created or last updated. You will find documents of all ages. The earlier guides are likely to be overtaken by the advances in web or HTML features.

There are many websites that are provided to share information and experiences in designing websites. For example, view the web page at: http://webdesign.about.com/mbody.htm.

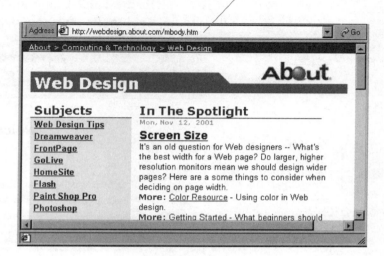

If it is programming the website that concerns you, there's a guide to all the HTML tags used by Netscape and Internet Explorer at http://werbach.com/barebones, which you can view or download.

Jakob Nielsen's "Writing for the Web" covers general web writing guidelines and practices, emphasising the different characteristics of printed and screen-based text. Visit:

www.sun.com/smrc/web/ writing/

See also his Web Usability site at:

www.useit.com/

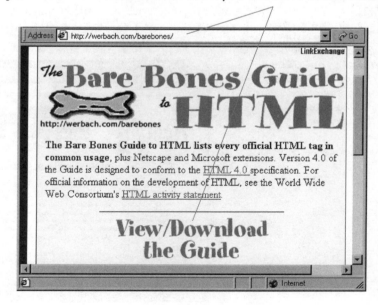

FrontPage user groups

The FrontPage User Group of New York emphasises "Plain English" design and technical information. Visit the site at http://www.frontpageusers.org. Membership is informal, and you can even join their extended community of users using Yahoo!Groups at http://groups.yahoo.com/fpug.

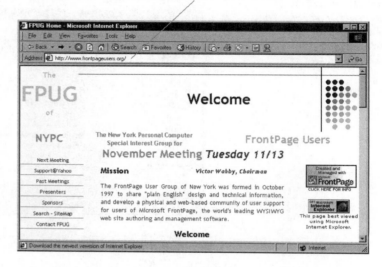

The UK FrontPage User Group (http://www.fug.co.uk) is rather more formal, with a monthly magazine and an annual membership fee (£125 + VAT for individual members).

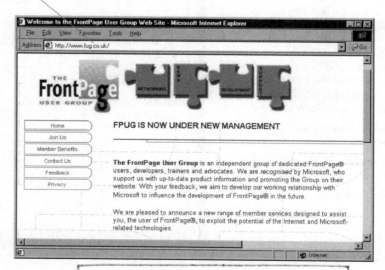

Index

E

Email 8, 12
Exchanging mail 8
Excite 106

F

Feedback 72–73
Folder list 45
Folders button 44
Folders view 20, 44
  Arranging files and folders 68–69
  No navigation bars 69
  No shared borders 69
Formatting buttons 43
Formatting toolbar 24, 43
Forms 91, 98–99
  Adjusting 74
  Form results
    Displaying 124–125
  Text boxes 73
Frames 58, 138–139, 147
  Alternate text 143
  Converting to 140–141
  Inline 143
    Defined 142
  No support for 144
  Older browsers 141
  Opposed to navigation bars 137
  Pages 58, 138
  Table of Contents 139, 141
  Templates 138
Freeserve 103
FrontPage 7, 13
  Assistance 176
  Bulletin 181, 183
    Registering for 182
  Closing down 38
  Features 14, 16–17, 24
  Installing 21–22
    File types 41
  New York Personal Computer User Group 186
  Requirements 15
  Restarting 38
  Starting 24
  Tutorial
    Running 25
  Upgrading 21
  User groups 186
  Views 20
  Webs 18
  Websites 184
  World 184
FrontPage Server Extensions 88, 116, 131, 155, 171–172
FTP 19, 88–90

G

Go search engine 112
Graphical navigation 65
Guest books 10, 91, 134

H

Headings
  Formatting 56–57
Help 24, 173
  Internet-based 175, 177
    From Microsoft websites 181
  Local 174
  Other sources 17
  With FrontPage 176
Hit counters 10
  Adding 116
  Resetting 117
Hotspots
  Creating 166–167
    From text 168
  Defined 166
HTML 8, 41, 138, 163, 182, 185
  Code 13, 35
  Edit 13, 17
  Graphical tags 34–35
  Heading styles 56
  Language 52
HTTP 88, 96
Hyperlinks 32
  Broken 68, 85, 88

Standard toolbar   24
Status   24
Subwebs. *See* Web: Subwebs

T

Tables
   Converting text to   163
   Creating   160–161
      Within other tables   164–165
   Drawing   162
Tasks   17, 81
   Assigning   81, 83
   Creating   83
   Marking as completed   82
   Priority   81
   Renaming   81
   Showing task history   83
Tasks view   20
Text
   Adding/formatting   42–43
   Converting to tables   163
   Hyperlinks   53
   Plain
      Inserting   40–41
Themes   16, 43, 55, 63
   Adding new pages   70
   Applying   41, 67
   Bullets   63
   Buttons   63
   Colour   63
   Customising   66–67
   Fonts   63
   Graphical
      Applying   63–64
   Override manual format   64
   Pictures   63
   Previewing in browsers   63
   Renaming   67
Time stamp. *See* Web: Web pages: Adding a time stamp
Title bar   24
Toolbars
   Adding/removing buttons   43
Tutorial. *See* FrontPage: Tutorial: Running
   Folder   42

U

Undo button   59
URLs   8, 12
   Relative   45
   Shortcuts   54
   Volatility   184
Useful links   52

V

Video   8, 15
Views bar   20, 24, 40, 44
Virtual domain names   12
Visual Basic   17

W

Web
   Accessing   9
   Adding files to   44–45
   Browsers
      Internet Explorer   9, 15–16, 36
      Netscape   9, 16
   Connecting to   8
   Design   19
      Data for the Web   38
      Default page   30
      Defining the requirements   19
      Guides   185
      Positioning   135
      Scroll bars   146–147
      Setting the page size   146–147
      Specifying the structure   148
      Table structure   135
   Editing remotely   156–157
   Help on   175
   Home pages   8
      Aligning items on   33